Islamic Law, Theology, and Practice

Also by Ahmed Lotfy Rashed

What Would a Muslim Say?
Top 15 Tough Questions on Islam
The Qur'an Discussions
Interfaith Dialogues and Debates

Islamic Law, Theology, and Practice
What Would a Muslim Say?
Volume 4

by

Ahmed Lotfy Rashed

Common Word Publishing
"With Dialogue Comes Understanding"

Copyright

Copyright © 2018 by Ahmed Lotfy Rashed

All rights reserved. This book or any portion thereof may not be reproduced or used in any manner whatsoever without the express written permission of the publisher, except for the use of brief quotations in a book review.

Editing: Allister Thompson

Cover Design: Stewart Williams

ISBN–13: 978-0-9994318-2-5

Dedication

In the Name of God,
the Most-Gracious,
the Ever-Merciful.

Acknowledgments

There are many people to thank for this book:

First, I thank my mother for teaching me always to be patient, even if it is uncomfortable. And I thank my father for teaching me always to be truthful, even if it is unpopular.

Second, I thank my wife for her patience, support, and encouragement as I navigated each conversation.

Last but certainly not least, I want to thank the shining models whom I consulted or referenced for the more nuanced or detailed answers that I had to provide: Yasir Qadhi, Gai Eaton, Zaid Shakir, Hamza Yusuf, Nouman Ali Khan, Suhaib Webb, Sherman Jackson, Jeffrey Lang, Mustafa Akyol, Reza Aslan, and Jamal Badawi. May God bless you all and preserve your teachings for all students of Islam.

Contents

Copyright iv
Dedication v
Acknowledgments vi
Contents vii
Introduction 3
    Deep Conversations about Islam 4
The Atheist Debates 7
    Why Does Islam Call Itself "God's Religion?" 8
    Salvation and Guidance in Islam 13
    Women's Testimony 21
    Islam and Slavery 23
    Adoption in Islam 26
    Muhammad and Aisha 29
    Muhammad and Aisha: Part 2 32
    No Compulsion in Religion? 40
The Philosopher Dialogues 59
    The Problem of Evil 60
    The Question of Euthyphro 66
    An Alternative Theology of God 75
    A Muslim Reformation? 80
Why Islam? 87
    Islamic Theology and History 88
    Islamic Theology and History: Part 2 96
    The Muslim Lifestyle 109
    Prayer and Friendships 114
    Understanding the Prophetic Traditions 117

A New Beginning	129
A Message From the Author	132
About the Author	xi
Appendix A	xii

TOUGH QUESTIONS AND HONEST ANSWERS ABOUT THE WORLD'S FASTEST-GROWING AND MOST CONTROVERSIAL FAITH

TOP 15 TOUGH QUESTIONS ON ISLAM

AHMED LOTFY RASHED

Get your FREE copy when you sign up to the author's email list!

**GET IT HERE:
WhatWouldAMuslimSay.net**

MY TEACHER WAS AHMED RASHED. WE SPENT A LOT OF TIME GOING THROUGH THE QUR'AN. AFTER THAT I STARTED TO UNDERSTAND MUSLIMS MUCH BETTER.
—A FORMER ISLAM-101 STUDENT

Islamic Law, Theology, and Practice

INTRODUCTION

Introduction

Deep Conversations about Islam

This book contains conversations with people who reached out to WhyIslam.org for dialogue and received me as their correspondent. WhyIslam conversations typically begin when a person visits the WhyIslam website and submits a "One to One Email Correspondence" form. Once assigned, the questions or comments are delivered to my email, and I then initiate the first email to reach out and respond to the visitor's questions. The conversation flows from there.

This volume is a continuation of my third book, ***Interfaith Dialogues and Debates***, and contains three long, theological conversations with a skeptical atheist (2013), a philosophy and religious studies professor (2015), and a soul-searcher (2017). This volume discusses Islamic history, Islamic law and practice, and Islamic theology and philosophy. It showcases many of the postmodern critiques of Islam and the responses to those critiques.

The conversations in this book are real. They are faithful transcripts of email correspondence that I have had with WhyIslam.org visitors over the years. To protect the privacy of our visitors, the names and identifying details have been changed. That email is reproduced here for reference.

Standard Email Introduction

Email #01 – From: Ahmed Rashed

In the Name of God, the Most-Gracious, the Ever-Merciful:
Thank you for taking the time to contact us and learn about Islam straight from the source. We practice and promote a balanced view of Islam — the "middle way" that the Qur'an calls Muslims to follow: a path of moderation that is free of *extremism*.

Before we begin, let me introduce myself. My name is Ahmed Rashed. I was born in Egypt but raised in America. I am married with three little children. I work as a test software engineer, but my life passion is teaching others about Islam.

Now I'm going to give you a brief description of what Islam is all about: Islam is not a new religion. Rather, it is the same truth that God revealed through all His prophets to every people. For over a fifth of the world's population, Islam is both a religion and a complete way of life. Muslims are taught to be truthful, to be just, to help the needy, to honor their parents, and to maintain good relations with neighbors and relatives.

The Qur'an tells Muslims to say: **"We believe in God and what was revealed to us, and what was revealed to Abraham and Ishmael and Isaac and Jacob and the Tribes, and what was given to Moses and Jesus and to the Prophets from their Lord. We do not separate between them, and to Him we submit." (3:84)**

This is how Islam sees itself in relation to all other religions. The Message revealed to Muhammad is considered God's religion for humanity in its final form. Muslims view Muhammad as the final successor to Jesus, Moses, Abraham, and all the previous prophets. Muslims view the Qur'an as the final Testament from God to humanity. Just as God sent revelation to Moses and Jesus (peace be upon them), Muslims believe God sent revelation to Muhammad (peace be upon him) to confirm, correct, and complete all previous Scriptures.

The Qur'an says that God sent prophets to every community in history. These prophets were men of high moral character chosen by God to teach their people about their duty to God and to their fellow man. The Qur'an teaches that this duty was always "submission and devotion to God" and to treat all God's creation with equality and compassion.

"Islam" is simply the Arabic word for this duty of "submission and devotion" to God.

"Muslim" is the Arabic word for "one who submits" to God and obeys Him.

The Qur'an says that whenever a people broke away from God's teachings, God would send another prophet to bring them back to His Path. This is how Muslims understand the many prophets sent to the Children of Israel and the many religions in the world today.

Prophet Muhammad, like all the prophets before him, called people to believe in and worship One God, to believe in His angels, to believe in His prophets, to believe in His revelations, to believe in the Day of Judgment, and to believe in Divine Decree and Destiny.

Prophet Muhammad, like all the prophets before him, called people to bear witness that there is no god but God and that he was God's Messenger, to pray regularly, to give charity regularly, and to fast as a form of self-purification. Prophet Muhammad, like Prophet Abraham before him, called people to make the pilgrimage to the Holy Sanctuary in Mecca, where the first house of worship dedicated to God Almighty was built.

This is just a general overview, so please reply with any questions you may have. I look forward to your response, and I hope to continue the discussion.

May peace be with you,
Ahmed Rashed

THE ATHEIST DEBATES

The Atheist Debates

Why Does Islam Call Itself "God's Religion?"

Email #02 – From: Kayan
Sent: Monday, September 26, 2011 10:17 a.m.

I have a few questions around the verses in the Qur'an, and I hope you will be able to explain the rationale behind them.
1. Why is it claimed that Islam is the only true religion and that all other religions are false? If that is the case, how come Allah allows there to be more non-Muslims (Christians, Hindus, Buddhists, atheists, etc.) than Muslims in today's world?
2. **"There is no compulsion in religion."** This is an oft quoted verse from the Qur'an to convince people of the tolerance in Islam to other religions. If this is true, why does Allah eternally torture and punish non-Muslims?
3. If Islam stands for peace and coexistence with other religions, how can one justify Prophet Muhammad's destroying of idols in the Kaaba? How is that different from the recent Taliban bombing of the Bamiyan Buddha statues in Afghanistan?

Email #03 – From: Ahmed Rashed
Sent: Thursday, September 29, 2011 5:07 p.m.

In the Name of God, the Most-Merciful, the Most-Gracious.

These are very weighty questions. Please forgive me for the delay and the lengthy reply. We will address each of your questions in order.

1. The first part of the question is why Islam claims it is the only true religion. The second part is why Muslims should be outnumbered by non-Muslims if Islam is the so-called "truth."

We start by clarifying that our purpose is not to convert anyone. We merely present accurate information on Islam; after that, a person is free to accept or reject Islam as they wish. Having said that, let us look at the philosophy behind Islam's claim and its understanding of what it means to be "God's Religion."

Muslims believe that the Last Prophet (Muhammad) and the Last Testament (the Qur'an) were sent to confirm, correct, and complete the Message of all previous Prophets and scriptures.

It is written in the Qur'an: **And whoever seeks a religion other than *Islam*, it will not be accepted from him and he will be one of the losers in the Hereafter. (3:85)**

This seems extreme, but it is written in the Qur'an that God made a covenant with every people in every time. This covenant was *"Islam,"* which means "surrender and obedience to God," and a person who surrenders his will to God and obeys His commandments is called a *"Muslim."*

Whenever a people broke their covenant with God (i.e., stopped obeying God's commandments) or changed the teachings of the Prophet sent to them, God would send another prophet to bring them back to the True Path, the path of submission and obedience to their Creator. In Arabic, this is called "Islam." This is how we understand the many prophets sent to the Children of Israel. If a people were still on the correct teachings of a prophet, there is no need for God to send another one. It is only when a people go astray that God would send one who would guide them back to the Truth. This is also how we understand the many divergent religions of the world today. Many of them WERE originally inspired and sanctioned by God, but after that particular prophet died or was ascended to Heaven, the generations after him forgot, neglected, or changed those pristine teachings for man-made assumptions and philosophies.

So the original followers of Abraham are considered *Muslims* by virtue of their obedience to God and the keeping of their Covenant with Him. And the original followers of Moses are considered *Muslims* by virtue of their obedience to God and the keeping of their Covenant with Him. And the original followers of Jesus are considered *Muslims* by virtue of their obedience to God and the keeping of their Covenant with Him.

By the time of Muhammad (peace be upon him), there were few, if any, who were still upon the original, pure teachings of any prophet. So God sent Muhammad as the Final Messenger with the Final Revelation to guide the Arabs in particular and all of mankind in general to the correct path to their Lord and Creator. So the point is not to get hung up on the Arabic word *"Islam"* but rather understand what that Arabic word means: "submission and devotion to God." Whoever does that, at any time and in any place, will receive God's Mercy.

This is why the final Prophet of Islam (pbuh) said: *"Anyone who says 'There is no god but God' and dies holding that (belief) will enter Paradise."* Islam teaches that whoever follows the original teachings of the authentic prophets will find salvation, because all the prophets preached that God is ONE, distinct and separate from His creation, and that all worship deserves, by right, to go to Him alone. Muslims believe that only Islam still has the unadulterated authentic and original teachings of a real genuine Prophet of God; this is Islam's claim to truth. Obviously, there are other faith traditions and other truth claims, but that is for each human being to seek and decide for him- or herself.

So now this brings us to the second part of the question. If Islam is the so-called "truth," why are Muslims not the most dominant people on Earth? Why are they weak and outnumbered? There are two responses to this issue.

The first is that God does not "favor" anyone for any reason other than their merit and devotion to HIM. As a point of fact, when the Prophet died and the Companions expanded the Islamic Empire, nation after nation fell to the political power of the Muslim armies. More amazingly, people after people fell to the spiritual allure of Islam and embraced it in multitudes. This was seen by the contemporaries of the time as a sign of divine assistance. To wit: if Muslims are on the right path, God will grant them victory on earth and in the hearts of men; but if Muslims are on the wrong path (like Muslims today), God will not give them mastery over the earth or make them respected and sought after by the hearts of men. Muslim scholars teach us that you cannot rest on your past achievements with God; therefore, it is argued that the current weakness and small number of Muslims is a sign of Muslim sinfulness, not a sign of Islam's invalidity.

The second is that it is a mistake to assume God will make his true devotees and followers the uppermost at every instant in history. God's promise was that each *individual* believer will get his reward in the hereafter. God's promise to the COMMUNITY of believers is if the COMMUNITY believes and does righteous deeds, only then will God give them power and numbers on earth: **Allah has promised, to those among you who believe and work righteous deeds, that He will surely grant them power in the land, as He granted it to those before them; that He will establish in authority their religion — the one which He has chosen for them; and that He will change their state of fear in which they lived to one of security and peace: 'They will worship Me alone and not associate aught with Me.' If any do reject Faith after this, they are rebellious and wicked. (24:55)**

2. This question is asking how "no compulsion" is reconciled with eternal damnation in hellfire for disbelievers. We understand that "compulsion" means somebody forcing you to do something. God does not want people who worship him unless that worship is sincere. There are many well-known Sayings of the Prophet (*Hadith*) warning that worship without sincerity will be rejected on the Day of Judgment. Even the testimony of faith, that statement that brings a person into Islam, is INVALID if it is coerced or forced.

Having said that, Hell is the punishment for dying on disbelief after clear signs and messengers have come. **For those who did NOT receive clear signs or messengers, their test will be on the Day of Judgment.** There is no contradiction. Just as there is a punishment for sin, a person still has the free will to choose to sin or be good. That is the whole point of this life; it is a test of faith for each individual. There are many things besides disbelief whose punishment is Hell, but God still allows people to do them. There is no contradiction between "no compulsion in religion," which means that religion is only valid if it voluntary and "punishment for sin," which means that any voluntary transgression will be accounted for.

3. These situations are different. Muhammad (pbuh) was sent, in part, to cleanse the House of God that Abraham had built over four thousand years ago. The idols were desecrating a previously standing known temple dedicated to the One and Only God. So his destroying the idols was justified. What the Taliban did is not the same because the Companions of the Prophet did not destroy the Sphinx of Egypt or the Arch of Ctesiphon or the icon-filled Churches of Jerusalem. Did the Companions not have as much faith or zeal as the Taliban? Did they not have as much power? They had conquered all these lands and had its people under their thumbs; they could have done so if they wished, but they did not. They understood what Islam actually stands for and which acts were to be emulated by Muslims in general and which acts of the Prophet were for him alone. The Taliban do not always demonstrate understanding of these subtle nuances.

May peace be with you,
Ahmed

Salvation and Guidance in Islam

Email #04 – From: Kayan
Sent: Friday, September 30, 2011 8:43 a.m.

Salaam,
The Qur'an is clear about the punishment that Allah has in store for non-Muslims, just on the basis of their faith. By these verses, a person of the standing of Mahatma Gandhi or Mother Teresa will go to hell just because they believe in gods other than Allah. Why is it that their deeds are not taken into account? According to [other] verses, it is Allah himself that has sealed the hearts, ears, and eyes of the disbelievers and then sends them to burning Hell for their faith; how does this reconcile with the premise of a merciful and loving god?

Email #05 – From: Ahmed Rashed
Sent: Monday, October 10, 2011 2:17 p.m.

In the Name of God, the Lord of Mercy, the Ever-Merciful:
To begin, Allah is simply the Arabic word for "The God," so I will use Allah and God interchangeably in our discussion. There are three separate topics that this question addresses:

A. Why is Islam called a religion of tolerance?

B. Why is it that the good deeds of disbelievers are not taken into account?

C. How is it fair for God to punish disbelievers when He says that He leads them astray?

A. TOLERANCE

This topic confounds two separate issues as if they were related or interdependent.

1. To say that "Islam is a religion of tolerance" means that the religion of Islam teaches its followers, the Muslims, to be fair, kind, and cordial to followers of other religions.

2. To say that "God will punish those who died as disbelievers" means that the religion of Islam teaches that God has certain acceptance criteria for how He will judge humanity on the Day of Judgment and that the one most critical criterion is correct faith/belief in God.

These two statements are not contradictory. I can easily say in one breath that God will punish disbelievers in the hereafter but also that God has commanded us to treat disbelievers with excellence and fairness in the here and now.

Islamic doctrine holds that human existence continues after the death of the human body in the form of spiritual and physical resurrection. There is a direct relation between conduct on earth and the life beyond. The afterlife will be one of rewards and punishments that are commensurate with earthly conduct. A Day will come when God will resurrect and gather the first and the last of His creation and judge everyone justly. People will enter their final abode, Hell or Paradise. Faith in life after death urges us to do right and to stay away from sin. In this life we sometimes see the pious suffer and the impious prosper. All shall be judged one day, and justice will be served.

Islam teaches that people will be resurrected body and soul to be judged by God according to their faith and deeds. Paradise is for those who dedicated their worship only to God, who continuously sought His forgiveness, and who lived moral lives according to the authentic teachings of their Prophet and Scripture. Hell is the final dwelling place of those who denied God, worshiped other beings besides God, or rejected the call of the Prophets.

Hell is also the temporary abode of those who had faith but led sinful, unrepentant lives. This is because the Qur'an says: **Surely, God will not forgive the ascribing of partners to Him. But He forgives whoever He will for anything other than that. Whoever ascribes partners to God has strayed far indeed. (4:116)**

So those who had faith but led sinful, unrepentant lives will be punished in Hell until their sins have been purged and their souls have been purified. Once this purification is complete, by God's mercy they will be taken out of Hell and admitted into Paradise.

This is because the Qur'an tells us that the whole REASON why God created people on this earth was so they could know God. This worldly life is just a test to see who would seek to know God, and from this knowledge, love God, and from this love, worship and serve God on HIS terms, not ours. Therefore, a person who denies God or refuses to worship Him as He has commanded has failed to fulfill his purpose of existence.

Having said all that, a person who denies God still has all the rights to life, wealth, family, honor, and intellect that a Muslim has. These are fundamental human rights in Islamic law, regardless of whether a human being believes or disbelieves. So a disbeliever has the right to "live their life," but Islam teaches that the final state of such a person is not the same as one who believes.

The Qur'an says:

There is no compulsion in faith. (2:256)

If your Lord had so wished, all would have believed; will you then force people to believe? (10:99)

Say, "This is Truth from your Lord": Let he who wishes believe, and let he who wishes reject. (18:29)

The Qur'an says: **God does not forbid you, regarding those who have not fought you in religion's cause, nor expelled you from your homes, that you should be kindly to them, and act justly towards them; surely God loves the just. God only forbids you as to those who have fought you in religion's cause, and expelled you from your homes, and have supported in your expulsion, that you should take them for allies. And whosoever takes them for allies, those are the evildoers. (60:8-9)**

So non-Muslims who do not fight against our faith or drive us from our homes should be treated with goodness and equality.

The Prophet said, *"Whoever hurts a non-Muslim citizen of a Muslim state hurts me, and he who hurts me offends God"* and, *"He who hurts a non-Muslim citizen of a Muslim state, I am his adversary; and I shall be his adversary on the Day of Judgment"* and, *"Anyone who kills a non-Muslim who has a pact of peace with us will not smell the fragrance of Paradise."*

From this, Islamic scholars are unanimous that the life, property, and honor of non-Muslims who do not attack Muslims or drive them from their homes are as sacred as the life, property, and honor of Muslims.

That is what tolerance means. It means that even though I believe what you are doing is wrong and that you will be held to reckoning because of it, I still treat you with good words and kind acts. God alone judges men, so God alone has the right to punish men for their disbelief in Him. This is not intolerance; this is God's right as *The Law-Giver* to make commandments and His right as *The Reckoner* to punish people in the hereafter for failing to obey His commandments.

So in conclusion, the issue of hereafter punishment of disbelievers by God is separate and independent from the issue of righteous treatment toward disbelievers by believers. Therefore, we contend that despite the verses quoted in the initial question, Islam **is** a religion of tolerance because it **explicitly** teaches in both Qur'an and Hadith that Muslims must treat peaceful non-Muslims with honor, fairness, and excellence.

B. SALVATION

What are the requirements of salvation? Why is it that even a good person would go to hell for being an atheist or a believer in Trinity or a believer of multiple gods?

We have already said in the previous section that God has rights, and His most important right is that we worship Him and only Him. This is the first commandment: **"Thou shalt have no other gods before God."** This is the creed of Islam and of all the Prophets before Muhammad: *"O People, know that your god is One God, and He has decreed that you worship none but Him."*

We start the new discussion with the fact that the good deeds of the disbelievers **are,** in fact, taken into account. The key to Paradise is belief in God as ONE, without partners, children, or demigods.

With that key of right behavior toward the **Creator**, you are allowed to enter Paradise, and then the right/wrong behavior you had toward the **creation** will determine your final level of reward in paradise. More right behavior means more reward. More wrong behavior means less reward. But God alone knows this and God alone decides.

Without that key of right behavior toward the **Creator**, you are not allowed to enter Paradise, so you enter Hell, and then the right/wrong behavior you had toward the **creation** will determine your final level of punishment in Hell. More right behavior means less punishment. More wrong behavior means more punishment. But God alone knows this and God alone decides.

We can think of two analogies to clarify this concept:

1. Employers hire workers to fulfill certain tasks. No matter how well a worker treats his coworkers or takes care of the store, if a worker fails to do the tasks *for which he was hired*, the employer will fire that worker when it is time to do performance evaluations. While it is true that this worker would be appreciated for his service to coworkers, that worker will not be allowed to progress in the status, compensation, or even presence of the employer.

Likewise, God created humanity to acknowledge Him and worship only Him. So disbelievers (whether atheist, polytheist, or trinity-believer) have failed to fulfill the purpose for which they were created. Therefore, disbelievers will not be able to progress in status with God, compensation from God, or even presence of God when it is time to do performance evaluations, a.k.a. the Day of Judgment.

2. Teachers expect students to learn certain things. No matter how well a student treats his classmates and takes care of the classroom, if a student fails to demonstrate *the subjects he was supposed to learn*, the teacher will fail that student when it is time

to do final grades. While it is true that this student would be appreciated for his service to classmates, that student will not be allowed to progress to the next level.

Likewise, God created humanity to know Him and to learn about His exalted nature and His majestic attributes. Disbelievers have failed to demonstrate practical understanding and appreciation of God, His Nature, His Attributes, and His right to be worshiped and praised as He commands, not according to their own ideas and whims. Therefore, disbelievers will not be able to progress to the next level with God — which is living in the presence of God's Radiance and Beneficence in Paradise.

As for those who never met a prophet or received clear and accurate information about the True Path, I already said in my previous message that God will test them on Judgment Day.

C. GUIDANCE

What is the nature of human free will? What is the nature of God's power over and knowledge of His creatures? Why is it that the Qur'an mentions guiding and "misguiding?"

People are responsible for their actions. If this were not the case, then punishing the wicked would be unjust, and rewarding the righteous would be a joke. God does not jest, and He did not create this world as some form of amusement. In addition, it is written many times in the Qur'an that **"Never is God unjust to His creatures."** So we conclude that human free will is genuine.

God's power and knowledge over His kingdom is absolute. Nothing happens without his knowledge, permission, and power. So "the buck stops with Him." There is no one who can do something outside of His will. For this reason, people and events are called *"asbaab,"* which is Arabic for "causes," but God is called *"al-musabbib,"* which is Arabic for "the causer." So in this sense, He is the ultimate decider of what happens on earth. However, His decision takes into account the free will, intention, and agency of human beings. For this reason, the Qur'an mentions that God has *allowed* people to go astray.

It is NOT the case that God is the active cause of their disbelief and hypocrisy, rather it is that God is sublime and gives everyone what they are striving for. He who exerts effort to get closer to God will be guided and helped, and his repentant urges will be amplified. He who exerts effort to turn away from God will be left to his choice, and his sinful urges will be amplified.

This concept of evil intentions collapsing on the perpetrator is a common theme in the Qur'an. So the Qur'an talks about God *"increasing the disease in their hearts"* and *"plotting against their plots"* and *"turning their mockery back upon them."* God is *Al-Aziz*, which figuratively means "the Almighty" but literally means *"the Unbeatable."* The point is that God cannot be fooled, tricked, or frustrated, not that He "is out to get mankind." He is far above such descriptions.

When you study the names and attributes of God, "the Deceiver," "the Plotter," and "the Mis-Guider" are not among them. Rather it is Satan who is called "the Deceiver." So how do we understand the verses that say God deceives the deceivers, or that God plots against the plotters, or that God misguides the misguided? The answer is that God takes the evil intentions of deceivers and plotters and the misguided and turns them back upon them. So God does NOT deceive Man, but He allows those men who deceive others to have a false sense of security regarding God's judgment. God does NOT plot against Man, but He allows evil plots to fall in on the heads of the evil plotters. God does NOT misguide Man, but He allows those who stubbornly cling to misguidance to continue going further and further astray.

This is the understanding of hypocrisy and disbelief. This attitude is condemned in the Qur'an, and that is why God reproaches them and warns them that continuing this path will cause them to fall out of God's grace and mercy and instead make them worthy of His wrath and curse. So those who persistently disbelieve and do evil on earth will find their destiny forever dark.

This is why the Qur'an says: **And remember, Moses said to his people: "O my people! Why do ye harm me, though ye know that I am the apostle of Allah (sent) to you?" Then when they went wrong, Allah let their hearts go wrong. For Allah guides not those who are rebellious transgressors. (61.5)**

However, anyone who sincerely turns to God will find God responsive and forgiving. God does not "send" anyone astray, Kayan. Rather, He "leaves" astray those who refuse guidance from Him. Anyone who sincerely seeks God will be guided by Him: **God chooses whoever He pleases for Himself and guides towards Himself those who turn to Him. (42:13)**

The first part of 42:13 is "special Grace," which means God choosing and guiding a person even if that person was far away from God. This is a gift from God independent of what the person does *vis-à-vis* God. The second part of 42:13 is "common Grace," which means God's responding to and guiding any sincere seeker of God. This is a promise from God in response to what the person does *vis-à-vis* God.

Finally, it is written that **"God does not desire disbelief for his servants,"** so we know that any who transgress will be allowed to transgress by their own free will, not by God "forcing" them to transgress and then punishing them for that transgression. Just as God created us so that our intellects should supersede our emotions and desires, so too God's Will and Revelation should supersede our intellects. This worldly life is a test: Can you use your intellect, reasoning, and free will to **acknowledge** the *limitations* of your intellect, reasoning, and free will? Therefore, can you submit your intellect, reasoning, and free will to your Creator?

May peace be with you,
Ahmed

Women's Testimony

Email #06 – From: Kayan
Sent: Friday, September 30, 2011 8:43 a.m.

Salaam,
The Qur'an (2:282) talks about women being accorded half the intellectual standing of men. Although this may have been the accepted norm in the 6th century, it is no longer applicable today.
I would really appreciate your views on the above verses.

Email #07 – From: Ahmed Rashed
Sent: Wednesday, October 12, 2011 4:33 p.m.

In the Name of God, the Lord of Mercy, the Ever-Merciful:
The Qur'an does NOT state that a woman's intellect is worth half a man. The verse above merely says that when writing a contract of deferred debt, two men are preferred, and if two men cannot be found, then one man and two women.

This verse is understood to be advisory, not regulatory. That means that it is a recommendation, not a binding command. The scholars understand this because there is a general rule in Islamic jurisprudence that states: *"If there is a command in the Qur'an that the Prophet sometimes did not implement, then the command is understood to be a suggestion or advice from the Creator to Humanity."* It is a known fact that the Prophet sometimes made a contract for deferred debt without any witnesses at all; therefore, this verse is just advisory (an advice for the time and place revealed) and **not** regulatory (a law to be binding on all people and all times). So as you said, it does not apply today.

As for why this verse was revealed in the Prophet's time, since financial responsibility was shouldered by men, they were expected to be well-versed in financial transactions, as compared with women. As a second option, the witness can be one man and two women, so that if one of the women errs the other can remind her. The Arabic word used in the Qur'an is *'Tadhil,"* which means "to confuse" or "to err." Many have wrongly translated this word as "to forget." Thus, financial transactions constitute the only case in which two female witnesses are equal to one male witness, and even then, only in cases where the financial experience of women is less than that of men, as was the case in 7th century Arabia.

There are some scholars who are of the opinion that the rule of two female witnesses equal to one male witness should be applied to all the cases. This cannot be agreed upon because one particular verse of the Qur'an from Sura Noor, chapter 24, verse 6, clearly equates one female witness and one male witness.

In addition, it is well known that a **single woman's testimony** was accepted as decisive in cases of adultery, rape, theft, murder, determining the start of Ramadan, and narrating the Sayings of the Prophet. Clearly, these cases are more serious than witnessing a financial contract for deferred debt, so the intellectual capacity of women to bear witness and relate information must be upheld as being equal to that of a man insofar as her individual memory and intelligence are concerned. This is the same as any man giving testimony. The trustworthiness of the testimony of a witness is directly proportional to the character and intellect of that witness (male or female), the more trustworthy their testimonies. So there is no difference.

May peace be with you,
Ahmed

Islam and Slavery

Email #08 – From: Kayan
Sent: Friday, September 30, 2011 8:43 a.m.

Salaam,
The next verses for discussion deals with treatment of slave women in captivity: **Successful indeed are the believers; those who are humble in their prayers, and those who shun vain talk, and those who pay alms to the poor; and those who guard their chastity — except from their wives or those whom their right hands possess (slaves), for them there is no blame. (23:1-6)**

My question deals with the validity of allowing sexual relations with slaves captured in war. How is such an act justified in any context?

Email #09 – From: Ahmed Rashed
Sent: Sunday, October 9, 2011 9:44 a.m.

In the Name of God, the Lord of Mercy, the Ever-Merciful:
First of all, this question has an underlying implication that sex between master and slave was not consensual and therefore constitutes rape. This is not the case. Islam forbids one to harm those under his authority. The Prophet (peace be upon him) made it clear that masters shouldn't harm their slaves:

Sahih Bukhari, Volume 1, Book 2, Number 29: *At Ar-Rabadha, I met Abu Dhar who was wearing a cloak, and his slave, too, was wearing a similar one. I asked about the reason for it. He replied, "I abused a person by calling his mother with bad names." The Prophet said to me, 'O Abu Dhar! Did you abuse him by calling his mother with bad names? You still have some characteristics of ignorance. Your slaves are your brothers, and Allah has put them under your command. So whoever has a brother under his command should feed him of what he eats and dress him of what he wears. Do not ask them (slaves) to do things beyond their capacity (power) and if you do so, then help them.*

The Prophet (peace be upon him) said that our slaves are like our siblings. Who would rape his own sister? The Prophet (peace be upon him) forbade causing physical harm to slaves:

Sahih Muslim, Book 015, Number 4082: *Hilal b. Yasaf reported that a person got angry and slapped his slave-girl. Thereupon Suwaid b. Muqarrin said to him: You could find no other part (to slap) but the prominent part of her face. See I was one of the seven sons of Muqarrin, and we had but only one slave-girl. The youngest of us slapped her, and Allah's Messenger (may peace be upon him) commanded us to set her free.*

If the Prophet (peace be upon him) forbade slapping slaves, then it's unthinkable that he would have permitted raping them. It just makes no sense. Since rape is a form of harm, it is obvious that rape is forbidden. This is not just my view, by the way. Below are statements of classical Muslim jurists.

Imam Malik said: *"In our view the man who rapes a woman, regardless of whether she is a virgin or not, if she is a free woman he must pay a 'dowry' like that of her peers, and if she is a slave he must pay whatever has been detracted from her value. The punishment is to be carried out on the rapist and there is no punishment for the woman who has been raped, whatever the case."* (Imam Malik, **Al-Muwata'**, Volume 2, page 734)

Imam Al Shafi'i said: *"If a man acquires by force a slave-girl, then has sexual intercourse with her after he acquires her by force, and if he is not excused by ignorance, then the slave-girl will be taken from him, he is required to pay the fine, and he will receive the punishment for illegal sexual intercourse."* (Imam Al Shafi'i, **Kitaabul Umm**, Volume 3, page 253)

Notice that both of these top classical scholars have stated that a man is to be punished for raping a slave girl. So this shows that the early classical scholars **understood** and **taught** that a master cannot force his slave girl to lie with him. Now, as for why the Qur'an even permitted this kind of relationship between master and slave girl, one must remember the cultural and historical context in which these verses were revealed.

In premodern times, a slave girl was the common-law wife of her master for all intents and purposes. This is not peculiar to Arabs or Muslims. This was the case in the east among the Indians and the Chinese. This was the case in the south among the African tribes. This was the case in the north among the Slavic tribes and in the Caucasus. This was the case in the west among the Byzantine Empire, the Roman Empire, and the European tribes.

The Qur'an did not invent slavery or the taking of slave girls as concubines, but it did regulate the treatment of slaves and enforced that they should be treated humanely and not abused.

> May peace be with you,
> Ahmed

Adoption in Islam

Email #10 – From: Kayan
Sent: Friday, September 30, 2011 8:43 a.m.

Salaam,

My next question deals with the status of adopted children according to the Qur'an: **Neither He has made your adopted sons as your own sons. These are merely words which you utter with your mouths: but God speaks the truth and gives guidance to the right path. Call them after their own fathers. That is closer to justice in the sight of God. If you do not know their fathers, regard them as your brothers in faith and your protégés. But there is no blame on you if you make a mistake therein. (What counts is) the intention of your hearts. And Allah is Oft-Returning, Most Merciful. (33:4-5)**

This effectively denies adopted children the rights that biological children have. Although I would agree that a child needs to know if he or she has been adopted, but that doesn't justify denying the right of a child to call his adopted parents as dad and mom.

Also, if you read the following verse, it seems to give the real reason why adopted children were denied the rights of biological children: **You said to the man who had been favored by God and by you, 'Keep your wife to yourself and have fear of God.' You sought to hide in your heart what God wished to reveal. You were afraid of people, whereas it would have been more proper to fear God. When Zaid divorced his wife, We gave her to you in marriage, so that there should be no restriction on believers marrying the spouses of their adopted sons when they have divorced them. The commandment of God must be fulfilled. (33:37)**

I would really appreciate your views on the above verses.

Email #11 – From: Ahmed Rashed
Sent: Friday, October 21, 2011 4:41 p.m.

In the Name of God, the Lord of Mercy, the Ever-Merciful:

The question of adoption in Islam is one that is very often misunderstood. Islam places a great emphasis on the ties of kinship; a completely abandoned child is practically unheard of. Islamic law would place an emphasis on locating a relative to care for the child before allowing someone outside of the family, much less outside of the community. This is to avoid removing the child from his or her familial, cultural, and religious roots. This is especially important during times of war, famine, or economic crisis, when families may be temporarily uprooted or divided.

The Prophet Muhammad (peace be upon him) once said that a person who cares for an orphaned child will be in Paradise with him, and he motioned to show that they would be as close as two fingers of a single hand. An orphan himself, Muhammad paid special attention to the care of children. He himself adopted a former slave and raised him with the same care as if he were his own son. However, the Qur'an gives specific rules about the legal relationship between a child and his or her adoptive family. The child's biological family is never hidden; their ties to the child are never severed.

Anyway, I am really surprised at your contention. The verse you quoted clearly says **(What counts is) the intention of your hearts.** So calling your adopted ward "son" or "daughter" out of affection is allowed. The same can be said for an adopted child calling the people who adopted him "father" and "mother" out of love and respect. This is perfectly fine. It is lawful to bring up children in one's house and to love them as one loves one's own children, but their attribution of those children should always be to their true, biological parents. If the identity of the child's parents is unknown, the child should be given a general attribution that originates with the child. So we see that what is unlawful is to attribute one's adopted child to oneself, as if there is a biological relationship.

This is because Islam seeks to safeguard biological lineage and not confuse lineage. The guardian-child relationship has specific rules under Islamic law, the point of which is to safeguard the rights of the orphans, not deny them! The relationship is somewhat different than what is common adoption practice today. In essence, it describes more of a foster-parent relationship.

These Islamic rules emphasize to the adoptive family that they are not taking the place of the biological family — they are trustees and caretakers of someone else's child. Their role is very clearly defined, but nevertheless valued, important, and protected.

As for your second contention, Zaid had been adopted as the Prophet's son. The Prophet's marriage to the divorced wife of Zaid was a practical demonstration that the adopted relationship was not equal to a real blood-relationship. A man cannot marry the divorced wife of his real son, but he can marry the divorced wife of his adopted son.

More importantly, before Islam, the Arabs did not allow divorcees to remarry. Zaid was adopted by the Prophet (pbuh) and called his son as was the custom among the Arabs before Islam. But Islam abrogated this custom and disapproved of its practice. Prophet Muhammad (pbuh) was the first man to express this disapproval in a practical way. So he married the divorcee of his "adopted" son to show that adoption does not really make the adopted child a real son of the adopting father and also to show that marriage is lawful for divorcees. This is what is meant by the end of the verse: **The commandment of God must be fulfilled.**

May peace be with you,
Ahmed

Muhammad and Aisha

Email #12 – From: Kayan
Sent: Friday, September 30, 2011 8:43 a.m.

Salaam,

The next narrative is from Bukhari's Hadiths and deals with Prophet Muhammad's marriage to Aisha: Volume 7, Book 62, Number 64: *Aisha narrates that the Prophet married her when she was six years old and he consummated his marriage when she was nine years old, and then she remained with him for nine years (i.e., till his death).*

How can one justify the consummation of marriage between a nine-year-old child and a fifty-three-year-old man? Although this might have been common practice in that day and age, I would have expected a Prophet to ban such practices as opposed to indulging in such practices himself.

Email #13 – From: Ahmed Rashed
Sent: Sunday, October 9, 2011 9:04 a.m.

In the Name of God, the Lord of Mercy, the Ever-Merciful:

Prophet Mohammad's youngest and only virgin wife was Aisha, the daughter of his life-long friend and companion. Her age at the time of marriage is NOT certain, because there are conflicting reports (each of equal authenticity) regarding when Aisha was born. The only thing that is certain is that their marriage was contracted about two years before the Migration to Medina and consummated about one year after.

According to one traditional Hadith source (the one you cited), Aisha was born eight years before the Migration, so she was six or seven years old when she was married to Muhammad and nine when the marriage was consummated.

However, other traditional sources disagree. Ibn Khallikan and Ibn Sa'd al-Baghdadi and Tabari report that **all** of Abu Bakr's four children were born before the Prophet's first revelation (610 CE), which means Aisha was at least twelve in 622 CE when the Muslims migrated to Medina. This implies that Aisha was thirteen or fourteen when the marriage was consummated.

In another traditional source, Aisha **herself** reported that, *"I was a young girl (jariya)"* when the 54th chapter of the Qur'an was revealed. It is known from other sources that the 54th Surah of the Qur'an was revealed **five years** before the Migration. Therefore, according to this tradition, Aisha had not only been born before the revelation of the referred chapter, but was actually a young girl at the time of this Surah's revelation. The Arabic word *"jariya"* refers to a girl between six to ten years old, so her age at consummation would have been at age twelve to sixteen.

In another traditional source, Aisha is reported to have died in the 58th year after Migration, when she was seventy years old. This implies she was twelve or thirteen when the Muslims migrated to Medina, and she was therefore thirteen or fourteen when her marriage was consummated.

Finally, other traditional sources report that Aisha's elder sister, Asma, was ten years older than Aisha. It is reported in **Taqreeb al-Tehzeeb** as well as in Ibn Kathir's **Al-Bidayah wal-Nihayah** that Asma died in the 73rd year after Migration when she was a hundred. Now, obviously if Asma was one hundred years old in the 73rd year after Migration, she should have been twenty-seven or twenty-eight years old at the time of Migration. If Asma was twenty-seven or twenty-eight years old at the time of hijrah, Aisha should have been seventeen or eighteen years old at that time. Thus, if Aisha was married about one year after Migration, she must have been between eighteen and nineteen years old when her marriage was consummated.

In conclusion, there are conflicting reports as to how old Aisha was when she married Prophet Muhammad. The sources point to age nine or age thirteen to fourteen (*the majority view*) or age sixteen to nineteen. What all the records agree upon is that Muhammad and Aisha had a loving and egalitarian relationship, which set the standard for reciprocity, tenderness, and respect enjoined by the Qur'an. Insights into their relationship, such as the fact they liked to drink out of the same cup or race one another, indicate they had a deep connection, free of any exploitation. This marriage is justified for the following reasons:

(a) She reached the full age of puberty. This is the standard around the world for tribal societies. To this day, the Bedouin tribes of Arabia, the tribes of Papua New Guinea, and the Yanomami tribe of the Amazon Basin all have their girls marry as soon as they complete their first menstrual cycle. Tribal societies do not have "adolescence" as more developed societies do. They have "coming of age" which is between nine and twelve for girls and eleven and thirteen for boys. When boys and girls "come of age," they are considered adults and are allowed to participate in adult activities like sex and marriage.

Since Islam is for all people and all times, Islam does not impose an arbitrary minimum age for marriage. Instead it states that so long as the bride and groom are both physically mature (postpuberty) and their families agree to the union, that marriage is valid. Islam leaves the minimum marriage age to the custom of the society. Therefore, it is perfectly okay for a developed society to set that age according to their custom (sixteen or eighteen usually), just as it is okay for a tribal society to set that age according to their custom (nine or ten usually).

(b) The marriage happened 1,400 years ago, not today. At that time, their marriage was not considered strange or even blameworthy. The proof of this is that the enemies of the Prophet at that time did not criticize this marriage. They attacked him on many other issues, yet they didn't criticize his marriage to Aisha.

(c) Aisha indicated how happy and honored she felt to be married to Prophet Mohammad. If she were unhappy or miserable because of this marriage, she would not have narrated so many positive, instructive stories and sayings about him. She definitely would not have mentioned the love and tenderness that existed between them.

May peace be with you,
Ahmed

The Atheist Debates

Muhammad and Aisha: Part 2

Email #14 – From: Kayan
Sent: Wednesday, January 11, 2012 10:22 a.m.

Salaam, Brother,

Thanks for taking the time to address my questions. I appreciate your efforts. Your explanation tends to the belief that girls became mature and of marriageable age much sooner in those times than in today's world. I agree that it may have been normal behavior for men of Prophet Muhammad's age to consummate marriage with nine-year-old brides in the sixth century. What bothers me is the fact that a supposedly last Prophet of God would behave thus. I would expect the last Prophet of God to behave in a way so as to be a role model for all time, not just for his time and age.

Another point you make is that in sixth century Arabia, short life expectancy and malnutrition caused puberty at a lower age. Please note that we are talking of both biological and emotional puberty here. Emotional maturity may depend on the environment, but biological maturity surely doesn't. In sub-Saharan Africa, malnutrition is rife, and life expectancy is not that far away from sixth century Arabia. Are you saying that girls from sub-Saharan Africa become biologically mature at age nine?

Coming to the point of Aisha's maturity at the time of marriage, here is a Hadith from Bukhari which clearly shows that Aisha played with dolls after her marriage. I can't imagine that a woman ready for marriage in all aspects would play with dolls. This clearly proves that Aisha was a child at the time of marriage to Prophet Muhammad (pbuh)

Volume 8, Book 73, Number 151: Narrated Aisha: *I used to play with the dolls in the presence of the Prophet, and my girlfriends also used to play with me. When Allah's Apostle used to enter (my dwelling place) they used to hide themselves, but the Prophet would call them to join and play with me.* (Fath-al-Bari page 143, Vol.13)

The second point you made was that Abu Bakr gave away Aisha's hand in marriage to Prophet Muhammad (pbuh). The following Hadiths from Bukhari clearly disprove this notion:

Volume 7, Book 62, Number 18: Narrated Urwah: *The Prophet asked Abu Bakr for 'Aisha's hand in marriage. Abu Bakr said "But I am your brother." The Prophet said, "You are my brother in Allah's religion and His Book, but she is lawful for me to marry."*

So basically, even Abu Bakr was not 100 percent willing to get his child married to Prophet Muhammad (pbuh), but he obviously could not refuse the last Prophet of God!

Here is another Hadith that reveals that Prophet Muhammad (pbuh) dreamed of Aisha from a marriage perspective at the time she was an infant, which wouldn't be the case if it was only on Abu Bakr's insistence that he married Aisha.

Volume 7, Book 62, Number 57: Aisha narrates that the Prophet said: *"You were shown to me in a dream. An angel brought you to me, wrapped in a piece of silken cloth, and said to me, 'This is your wife.' I removed the piece of cloth from your face, and there you were. I said to myself. 'If it is from Allah, then it will surely be.'"*

I would really appreciate your explanation of these Hadiths. From an accuracy perspective, I only refer to Bukhari and Muslim that are considered as "authentic" by the Islamic world.

Thanks for your time, and I hope you will be able to clarify these questions about Islam and Prophet Muhammad (pbuh)

Email #15 – From: Ahmed Rashed
Sent: Tuesday, January 17, 2012 12:22 p.m.

In the Name of God, Most Gracious, Most Merciful:

First of all, it is NOT a certified fact that Aisha was nine when marriage was consummated. That is just one report. The majority of reports imply her age was thirteen or fourteen, so most historians accept the majority evidence. This is well within the norms of that time and even by the standards of twentieth century rural or tribal communities.

Now we will address your replies in reverse order:

The Hadith of the dream is authentic but irrelevant to the discussion. The Prophet **did not** have this dream when Aisha was an infant; I honestly don't know from where you got this totally wrong idea. Furthermore, it was not even the Prophet's idea in the first place. A woman named Khaulah Bint Hakeem (an early convert and old matron) that first suggested he marry Aisha because the Prophet and Abu Bakr were best friends. Khaulah made the suggestion first, then he saw the dream, and after that the Prophet asked Abu Bakr for Aisha's hand in marriage. The order of events matters, and it disproves your assumption.

The Hadith about Abu Bakr is authentic, but your conclusion is erroneous. The Qur'an says it is illegal to marry your mother, your daughter, your sister, your aunt, or your niece. The *only* reason Abu Bakr initially hesitated to the marriage is because he thought the declaration of brotherhood between him and the Prophet made his daughter Aisha the *niece* of the Prophet. That is why once the Prophet clarified that the brotherhood between them was of faith, not of blood; there was no hesitation at all.

As for the idea that no one would refuse the request of the Prophet, *this is simply not true*. The Prophet had approached two mothers to ask for their daughters to marry on behalf of the Companions Bilal and Julaybeeb. Both refused. The first mother later agreed to marry her daughter to Bilal, but the second mother never let her daughter marry Julaybeeb, despite the Prophet's high opinion of him. One woman complained to the Prophet that she wanted a divorce from her husband for no reason other than she thought he was ugly and was not attracted to him. Several times, he requested that she reconsider because the husband was crying over their separation, but the woman **never** agreed the Prophet's entreaty, and the pair were divorced. Another woman was contractually married to the Prophet, but she refused to consummate on the wedding night. Without any fuss or fight, he released her and let her go back to her family. This shows that there were men and women who would refuse a request from the Prophet. He was only human, like they were, and so long as there was no divine command behind his human request, they had the choice to accept or reject his requests.

As for the Hadith about the dolls, it is authentic but irrelevant to the discussion. This incident is after the marriage was contracted but before the marriage was consummated. Note that Aisha reported that the Prophet visited her **in her place.** Therefore, this event happened **after** she was betrothed but **before** she moved into the Prophet's dwelling. So my initial explanation stands: she was contractually married before puberty, but no sexual contact happened until after she was ready both emotionally and physically. This is a salient point. If the Prophet was "indulging," why did he wait three years to consummate? Why did he not consummate right away? The answer is simple to those who are not burdened by cultural bias: *he waited until Aisha was physically and emotionally ready to live with him as his wife.*

As for age of biological puberty, the short answer is yes. My grandmother married when she was thirteen and started having kids when she was fifteen. My wife's mother married when she was fourteen and started bearing kids that same year. She had actually fully developed two years before at age twelve. My wife's grandmother was married at age twelve; again this was after puberty, when she had the physical ability to have and enjoy sex and emotional readiness to be a wife. All these women were raised in the poor farming communities of Egypt's eastern rural district. None of these women asked for divorce, and in fact all expressed great love and affection for their older husbands. The smallest age gap was six years, and largest age gap was sixteen years. I have not studied any broad-based anthropological surveys of Third World populations, but my own family history and the family history of my wife show me that in really poor nonindustrial societies, it is normal for girls to develop physically and emotionally young compared to Western industrial societies and actually thrive and find fulfillment in these marriages.

As for your feelings of being bothered that the Last Prophet of God would "indulge" in such behavior, I must challenge you to define what is so indulgent? The man never chased after women or had any paramours or lovers when he was young and vigorous. He didn't marry until he was twenty-five. Tell me how many men do you know who abstained from sex until age twenty-five? He stayed faithful to this one wife who was fifteen years OLDER than him for twenty-six years, even though he lived in a society where it normal for men to marry multiple wives without any financial responsibility for them. After she died, he waited two or three YEARS without any female companionship at all. Even after that, he married a widow that was OLDER than him. A year after that, he married Aisha. Two or three YEARS after that, he consummated. Again, the timeline refutes your objections.

Was Aisha a prepubescent child? I have already asserted that she was not **when consummation happened**. All the reports state that Aisha went to live with the Prophet as His wife AFTER she had reached puberty. She and her parents fully consented to the marriage. There was no criticism issued, neither at that time nor subsequently by Muslims and non-Muslims for many generations. Hence, this was in accordance with the prevailing custom and the normative tradition of girls marrying at puberty.

Was the marriage immoral due to the age gap? There is no universal principle that says a man and his wife must be no more than six or twelve or eighteen or whatever years apart. That is just convention and custom of the time and place. So long as both parties **consent** and the parents of the girl **consent** and no one in the community **objects**, why would he have to justify anything?

What constitutes a valid marriage? There are four universal conditions that must be met for any marriage to be considered valid and moral in Islam. First, the bride and groom must personally agree to the match; if there is any hesitation or doubt, the marriage is void. Second, the guardians of the bride must consent to the match; this is because the woman is usually the weaker party in a marriage. Third, the bride must be physically and emotionally capable of being a wife; this is an iron-clad requirement in Islam. Fourth, the groom must be physically, emotionally, and financially capable of being a husband. The

Prophet's marriage to Aisha fulfilled all these universal conditions. Any other requirements depend on **cultural** norms, not *absolute* moral or ethical laws.

May peace be with you,
Ahmed

Email #16 – From: Kayan
Sent: Sunday, January 22, 2012 4:18 p.m.

Salaam, Brother Rashed,

There is a reason why most countries outlaw child marriage. Yes, even today, there may be instances of successful childbirth for girls aged twelve or thirteen or even lower, but it has been statistically proved that early childbirth has a much bigger prevalence of death or complications during childbirth for the mother. About your contention that the Bukhari Hadith was after the engagement, but before the marriage, here's another one from a Muslim who is also recognized as "authentic" by the Muslim community:

Book 008, Number 3311: *Aisha reported that Allah's Apostle (may peace be upon him) married her when she was seven years old, and he was taken to his house as a bride when she was nine, and her dolls were with her; and when he died she was eighteen years old.*

This Hadith clearly says that Aisha went to Prophet Muhammad's (pbuh) house with her dolls — which clearly disproves the notion that she was a mature, adult woman ready for marriage in all respects.

I fully agree with your contention that this was the acceptable custom at that time. I know it was normal at that time to marry off young girls to much older men, but now we know that it is not acceptable practice and has consequently been banned. If Prophet Muhammad (pbuh) was to be a role model for all time to come, he should have adhered to standards that are acceptable for all times, including today.

Thank you very much for your time and patience.
Salaam

Email #17 – From: Ahmed Rashed
Sent: Sunday, January 29, 2012 11:10 p.m.

In the Name of God, Most Gracious, Most Merciful:
Again, I will address your replies in reverse order:

As for your issue that what was acceptable in the past is no longer acceptable now, I have already addressed this issue. Your objection is based on local custom, **NOT** any universal moral law. The universal moral law as exemplified by the Prophet is that you only require the four conditions mentioned in my previous email. Islam is for all people and all times; Islam does not impose an arbitrary minimum age for marriage. Instead it states that so long as the bride and groom are both physically mature (postpuberty) and their families agree to the union, then that marriage is valid. Islam leaves the minimum marriage age to the custom of the society. Therefore, it is perfectly okay for a developed society to set that age according to their custom (sixteen or eighteen usually) just as it is okay for a tribal society to set that age according to their custom (nine or ten usually). If the bride is physically and emotionally ready for married, then who can say the marriage is immoral or indulgent?

As for this second Hadith about Aisha's dolls, it is irrelevant to the question at hand. The text says that she took her dolls with her, not that she was playing with them. I knew many girls in high school, college, and graduate university who still had their childhood dolls with them after moving out of their parents' house. In fact, some of them even took them out and played with them from time to time. In addition, I know Egyptian mothers in their twenties and thirties who still play with dolls. By your logic, these women are still juveniles unfit for marriage and child-bearing. There are grown men who play with little toy soldiers or video games or dress up in medieval reenactments, so does this mean they cannot be fathers? Is this a universal criterion that can be applied to all places and all times? No. As before, you are assuming that the prevailing cultural norms and customs are absolute standards.

Aisha was a precocious child and a sharp woman; her intellect was above average, and it shows in all the Hadith where she is mentioned. After the Prophet's death she never spoke of any coercion or regret at her marriage. Instead, she would often mention the love she felt for him, her genuine jealousy regarding his other wives, her pride at being the one wife he wanted to be reunited with in Paradise, and her longing to be with him in bed when he chose to spend the night praying instead. These are not the recollections of an abused or exploited child. These are the recollections of a woman who entered marriage with eyes fully open. She truly loved her husband and desired to be with him.

Finally, regarding your issue that many countries have outlawed marriage below a certain age, this is again an issue of culture. Some countries have an age of consent of eighteen. Others set the minimum age at sixteen. Still others set it at fourteen and twelve and ten. These ages are all arbitrary, so which one is universally "correct?" Islam says there is a law that is independent of time or place or culture. The universal moral law says that consent is tied to the emotional and physical maturity of the bride and groom. Any other limitation is a reflection of culture and custom, not morality or ethics.

May peace be with you,
Ahmed

The Atheist Debates

No Compulsion in Religion?

Email #18 – From: Kayan
Sent: Wednesday, January 11, 2012 10:22 a.m.

Salaam, Brother,

Thank you for your time and patience with me. May I put forward a few points of discussion?

Allah says in the Qur'an that he created mankind solely for his worship. If this statement is true, why would He create people in non-Muslim communities when He clearly understands that the environment a child grows up in shapes his or her outlook in life? If a mother willingly leaves her infant child to a community of cannibals and willingly lets him grow up in that environment, is she justified in blaming him for having a cannibalistic outlook in life? How is this different from what Allah is doing? Allah is all powerful — he doesn't even have to exert Himself; He just needs to say "be," and it will be. In that case, why would he willingly create more non-Muslims when He hates rejection of Islam the most? If I were to create an army of entities with the sole purpose of praising me, why would I ever program them to be capable of doing anything else? And why would I ever put them in an environment where they will undoubtedly learn concepts that I absolutely hate?

Coming to the second question about "no compulsion in religion," let me give you an analogy. A poor, unarmed man stands face to face with a fully armed, well fed soldier:

- The soldier asks the poor man to do his bidding.
- The soldier adds that the poor man is free to follow instructions or to disobey him.
- The soldier adds that he (the soldier) absolutely hates people that do not do his bidding and that he will torture them.

Now, the soldier has given the poor man a "choice" to follow or not to follow — but is it really a choice at all?

Email #19 – From: Ahmed Rashed
Sent: Sunday, January 29, 2012 12:05 p.m.

In the Name of God, Most Gracious, Most Merciful:
You said, *"If I were to create an army of entities with the sole purpose of praising me, why would I ever program them to be capable of doing anything else?"* But Islam teaches that God already created beings that are programmed to praise and worship Him; they are called angels. Human beings are a different creation; they can choose either to worship God or turn away from Him.

Moving on to your second question, let us go step by step. If we assume for the sake of argument that God, not society, is the basis of morality, is it logical for the good and evil actions to have equal merit or consequences in the Eyes of God?

May peace be with you,
Ahmed

Email #20 – From: Kayan
Sent: Sunday, January 29, 2012 6:02 p.m.

Salaam, Brother Ahmed,
So in essence what you are veering toward is that God is the standard of all things, and he cannot say anything that is not good, hence what He says must be good — just a roundabout way to say the same thing.

Which leads to the second point then — since all morality is from God, and Allah is the only god, and Muhammad is the final Prophet, all morality must stem from the Qur'an and Hadiths, at least the ones recognized as "authentic" by the Muslim community.

Here are some excerpts from the Qur'an and Hadiths about morality as implemented by Prophet Muhammad (pbuh). **Can you honestly tell me that these are all good?**
1. Stoning adulterers to death (from Bukhari).
2. Not allowing an adopted child to call his adopted father as father. I think that matters a lot to the child.

3. A fifty-three-year old man consummating marriage with a nine-year old girl. I know we talked about this in another set of emails, and you cited cultural bias — but if God is the source of all morality and the only God is Allah, then sixth century Arabian culture is the only standard of morality, even in today's world.
4. Saying that a woman is deficient in intelligence and religion and that a majority of the inhabitants of hell are women because they are ungrateful to their husbands. See this "authentic" Hadith: Narrated Ibn Abbas: *"After the Farewell Pilgrimage at the Eid prayer, the Prophet (Allah bless him and give him peace) walked past the men leaning on Bilal's arm, and came to the rows of women behind them. Bilal spread out a cloth and the Prophet (Allah bless him and give him peace) urged the women to be generous with their gifts of charity, for when he had been allowed a glimpse into the flames of Hell, he had noted that most of the people being tormented there were women. The women were outraged, and one of them instantly stood up boldly and demanded to know why that was so. 'Because,' he replied, 'you women grumble so much, and show ingratitude to your husbands. Even if the poor fellows spent all their lives doing good things for you, you have only to be upset at one thing and you will say, 'I have never received any good from you!' At that the women began vigorously to pull off their rings and ear-rings, and throw them into Bilal's cloth."*
5. Allowing men to have sex with their female captives of war.

Please let me know your views on the above statements — are they good or are they bad?

Thank you for your time and patience.

Salaam

Email #21 – From: Ahmed Rashed
Sent: Monday, January 30, 2012 10:31 a.m.

In the Name of God, Most Gracious, Most Merciful:

Salaam, Brother Kayan:

Before I get to your comments, let us first go back to basics:

1. The Prophet taught that there is a Supreme Being, the one and only God, who is the Master and Ruler of the universe.

2. The Prophet taught that God reveals His teachings through Angels in Heaven to Prophets on Earth.

3. The Prophet taught that there is a Day of Judgment, where God will reward and punish people according to their obedience to His will.

These are the fundamental concepts in Islam as explained by the Qur'anic revelations and the Prophetic sayings. As Muslims, we believe that God is our *Creator*; therefore, He knows us and our condition better than even we know ourselves. As Muslims, we believe that God is the *All-Wise*; therefore, He knows what is best for our souls, our lives, our families, and our societies. As Muslims, we believe that God is the Loving Guider; therefore, He sent down His commandments for our own benefit, and so we may realize our full potential, not for tyrannical, whimsical, or dictatorial motivations.

So even if we do not fully understand the wisdom behind some of God's commandments, the fact that the majority of His commandments have clear and plain wisdom behind them are enough for us to have trust and faith in all His commandments. God says often in the Qur'an that He is Man's benefactor, that He only wishes what is best for Man. So as Muslims who believe that the Qur'an really is from our Creator and that Muhammad really was commissioned and inspired by our Creator, we accept His Will as our guiding Will. Now I shall address your statements:

1. Muslims believe that this penalty is just and good, because it is a deterrent to an action that is so destructive to individuals, families, and societies. Since this penalty **can only be applied** when the adulterers are *caught in the act* by four witnesses or

they bear witness against themselves four times in confession, it is understood the *spirit* behind this law is to highlight the enormity of the sin, not to ruthlessly punish adulterers.
2. I already addressed the issue of adopted children. If you recall, I said that it is fine for the child to call his guardian "Dad," so your issue is a nonissue. Therefore, this rule is just and good.
3. I already addressed the issue of Muhammad and Aisha. The fact that the Prophet only consummated after puberty means that henceforth there is no blame or sin on tribal societies who usually marry their children at a young age. So long as the bride and groom are both physically mature (postpuberty) and their families agree to the union, then that marriage is valid. Islam leaves the minimum marriage age **to the custom of the society**, so the Prophet's example is just and good.
4. Most mainstream Muslims understand the Arabic nuances in this Hadith. They **do not** interpret the "deficiencies" mentioned to be a literal description of all women; rather, they understand this to be an admonition to some of the women around the Prophet. Muslims believe that this statement is just and good because it motivated the women to be merciful to their husbands and to support the defense of the city.
5. The Qur'an did not invent slavery or the taking of slave girls as concubines; it **DID** regulate the treatment of slaves and **enforced** that they should be treated *humanely* and *not abused*. As I said before, in premodern times, *a slave girl was simply the common-law wife of her master for all intents and purposes*. So this rule is just and good because it gave the slave girl the right to seek justice if she was not treated as well as her master's wife.

    May peace be with you,
    Ahmed

Email #22 – From: Kayan
Sent: Tuesday, February 21, 2012 1:18 a.m.

Salaam, Brother Rashed,

I apologize for the delay in responding.

So, by your contention, "good" is ultimately an attribute of Allah. "Good" is good only because Allah prescribes it making scripture the only objective moral standard of good vs. bad.

By this contention, are we saying that slavery is "good"? It is allowed in Islam. There is no express condemnation or banning of slavery in the Qur'an. Coming to your other rebuttals:

1. You justify this penalty as just and good, but then you also justify sexual relations between a man and his slave without marriage; do you not see these statements as contradictory? Here, we are not even getting into a discussion on the free will of a slave girl to "refuse" her master's sexual advances. This is highly doubtful given the fact that her entire family would have been killed and she herself forcibly taken captive.
2. About adoption, the verse in the Qur'an clearly states that a child must be called with his biological father's name, meaning he cannot be officially adopted as a child of his foster parents. Today's adoption laws give an adopted child the same rights as a biological child. Of course, the child needs to know that he has been adopted, but how moral is it to call the child by his biological father's name when it is quite possible that the child may have been born out of a rape or when the biological father has no interest in the child's upbringing? If lineage is the sole reason why this law was put in place, this is easily achieved by DNA testing — why deny the poor child's legal right just because he has a biological father that doesn't care about his welfare?
4. As regards the Hadiths about women being inferior in intelligence and religion to men, even after reading the entire Hadith with context, I don't see any figurative talk in here. Prophet Muhammad is simply providing reasoning as to why the majority of people in hell will be women.

5. Can you please tell me which Hadiths or verses expressly give women slaves the right to refuse their masters' sexual advances? While it is true the Qur'an asks the captors to feed, clothe, and provide shelter to the slaves (that is one of the better verses), but look at the entire context of things. If I rob a bank at gunpoint and then give some money back, am I doing good by giving some of the money back to the bank, or am I overall a bad person for robbing the bank in the first place?

Thank you very much for your time and patience.
Salaam
Kayan

Email #23 – From: Ahmed Rashed
Sent: Wednesday, February 22, 2012 3:02 p.m.

In the Name of God, the Lord of Mercy, the Ever-Merciful:

I have answered your questions to the best of my abilities, Kayan. Your replies to my rebuttals have brought forth no new information, nor have they uncovered any glossed-over issue.

You asked about adoption, and I gave you a straightforward response. All your complaints are baseless, since no Muslim or non-Muslim scholar interprets that verse as you have wrongly interpreted them.

You asked about the Hadith against women's intelligence and religion, and I gave you a straightforward response from respected scholars and educators in the Islamic world.

First of all, the Hadith is figurative, not literal. Secondly, the Hadith is about fundraising, highlighting how sinful it is to curse others, and employing playful banter to solicit an outraged response from the some of the women present. This is clear in the original Arabic. Numerous verses and other narrations stress that the reward of women equals that of men, even if their acts differ. So this particular narration is not meant literally but as an acknowledgment of the inordinate power women wield over men while ostensibly less active in the public and spiritual spheres.

The real import of the Hadith — spoken at the Farewell Pilgrimage — and its actual context was that the Prophet (pbuh) challenged the women that were present to realize that unless they helped raise money with their gold and jewelry, they would miss the reward of men waging jihad as well as show ingratitude. If **socially conservative** Saudi scholars do not interpret this Hadith as justifying the denigration of women, how can you?

You asked about the institution of slavery, and I also gave you a straightforward response that Islam stands against slavery as a mindset and that it set up rules to weaken the institution of slavery. Slavery was not outright abolished, because that would have created more chaos and iniquity *at the time of revelation*. Slavery was not only practiced in Arabia but, in fact, all over the world. Therefore, banning such an institution is **ineffective** unless there is multinational agreement against it (as happened in the nineteenth century). Instead, the Qur'an and the Prophet sought to undermine the **basis** behind slavery and outlaw inhumane treatment so that slavery could gradually disappear.

Anyone who reads how the Prophet and his Companions treated and freed slaves would see that. The continuance of slavery is due to the greediness of later generations, not due to any intrinsic immorality of the Qur'an or the Prophet. You may read these two links if you desire more details:

http://www.central-mosque.com/fiqh/slav1.htm
http://www.al-islam.org/slavery/3.htm

You asked about the consistency of allowing male masters have sex with female slaves, and I had already replied that Islam gave them the same status as common-law wives. A Muslim man is required to get consent from her because it is against Islamic law to harm either one's wife or one's slave. Obviously, rape is a form of harm, and slaves DID historically seek justice in the Islamic courts. If a Muslim violates this law, then it merely reflects on that man's sin, not that God approves of such behavior.

May peace be with you,
Ahmed

Email #24 – From: Kayan
Sent: Thursday, February 23, 2012 2:55 p.m.

Dear Brother Rashed,

Your response to adoption was straightforward — yes, but that does not make it logical? If, as you said, lineage was the biggest concern in denying an adopted child legal rights (as we understand adoption in America today), how do you explain the contradiction with Adam and Eve's children committing incest or Adam committing incest with his daughters, without which we would not have such a large population in the world today?

As for women's intelligence, I gave you the relevant Hadith which clearly talks of a simple conversation between Prophet Muhammad (pbuh) and some women in which he said that women were deficient in intelligence and religion. He did not give any context to the conversation, so why should you as an interpreter? Please scroll down and read the Hadith again.

Regarding slavery — yes, the Qur'an does talk about the benefits of freeing slaves, but it also talks about capturing slaves in wars. You say that if slaves were not captured in wars, there would have been societal chaos. Was there societal chaos in Germany or Japan after the Allied forces left after World War II, even though no slaves were captured?

Regarding adultery, are you saying that if I bring home a maidservant from Asia, feed and clothe her and provide for her, with her consent I can have sex with her even though I am married to someone else? How is that different from keeping a mistress? How is that not adultery?

I am not sure if you will respond to this email, hence I would like to take this opportunity to thank you for all the time and patience you have shown with me.

Peace

Email #25 – From: Ahmed Rashed
Sent: Thursday, February 23, 2012 11:55 p.m.

In the Name of God, the Lord of Mercy, the Ever-Merciful:
My dear Brother Kayan,
Your responses reveal that you have not closely paid attention to either the words that I wrote or the links I provided. Let me go through each point one by one again:

Regarding adoption; yes, it is logical. If a person is the biological product of one pair of parents, it is NOT LOGICAL to ascribe paternity to another pair. That is a simple biological statement. Ascribe love. Ascribe the title "son," "daughter," "dad," or "mom" as you wish. That is okay. But do not ascribe paternity. Paternity, logically and ethically, can only be ascribed to the actual parents whose union resulted in the birth of the child. That is logical and that is fair.

The legal rights of adopted children in America are only a small fraction of the legal rights of adopted children in Islam; therefore, I am quite amazed that you think the Islamic framework denies any rights to adopted children. They are entitled to the inheritance of their biological parents, even if those parents had no part in their upbringing. America's laws do not entitle them such unless the biological parents choose to give them a share. They are entitled to know from the beginning the identity of their real parents. America's laws do not entitle them to know unless their biological AND adopted parents permit them to know their identity. They are entitled to call their adopted parents "dad" or "mom," as you seem to care so sensitively about.

As for Adam and Eve, I don't quite understand what this has to do with the discussion. According to Midrashim tradition, they had children in batches of twins. Abel had a twin sister. Cain had a twin sister. God commanded Abel to marry the twin sister of Cain and Cain to marry the twin sister of Abel. Cain's jealousy against his brother began with this command because he found his own twin sister (Abel's bride-to-be) more attractive than Abel's twin sister (his bride-to-be).

This level of incest was permitted at the beginning to allow more generations to be born. With each new generation of Prophets, the rules for who is prohibited for marriage were updated by revelation. This is God's wisdom for changing certain aspects of lawful and unlawful as societies develop, and this is why the laws of Moses differ slightly from the laws of Jesus, which differ slightly from the laws of Muhammad.

In all cases, the paternity and maternity of all offspring is still maintained, so there is no contradiction. Cain and Abel and their children and their children's children and so on could trace their ancestry correctly. DNA testing is dependent on time, place, and technology; universal laws should not depend on those. The American urbanite and the Australian Aborigine should all be able to follow the same guidelines if they are truly universal.

As for women's intelligence, I read the Hadith. *Did you study the historical context of this Hadith?* **Did you study the rest of the Hadith of the Prophet, where he would admonish a group of people when his intention was to correct the behavior of a few??** That was the Prophet's style. He could have singled out the few women who were being ungrateful to their husbands and stingy with their donations, but he did not because he was sensitive to the feelings of others. For this reason, knowing the style and methods of the Prophet from the corpus of Sayings that we have, the mainstream scholars from East and West do NOT conclude that women are intrinsically inferior to men. Therefore, your entire argument falls on its face.

Even if we use the most traditional or conservative interpretation, this Hadith uses *"majaz mursal."* This means using the whole for the part. So intelligence means the specific legal testimony of a woman, not intellectual capability in general; and religion means specifically the prayer and fast at the time of menses, not religiosity or piety in general. More importantly, what is translated as "deficiency" is more appropriately understood (even by conservative or traditional scholars) to mean "less responsibility," not "less capability."

On average, a woman will pray one week less per month than a man due to her menses, so this is "less responsibility," not "less capability," because after menopause, the woman will pray all month long. Likewise, a woman's testimony will be given half the weight of a man's only in the case of informal deferred debt, and even then, as mentioned in our previous conversation, only on an optional advisory basis, not a mandatory statutory basis. So this is "less responsibility," not "less capability," because for any other case, a woman's testimony is equal to that of a man.

Regarding slavery, I did not say "if slaves were not captured in wars, there would have been societal chaos." What I said was that one of the wisdoms behind Islam not banning slavery as an institution is because outright abolishment of that worldwide institution would cause more problems than it solves. You assume that "banning" would have been effective, but ask any historian of the American Civil War how African Americans in the South still faced rampant injustices and attacks on their liberty. After the Reconstruction, whites imposed laws to prevent them from voting, restrict their movement, and found other ways to practice involuntary servitude. This prompted journalist Douglas A. Blackmon to write in his Pulitzer Prize-winning book **Slavery By Another Name** that many blacks were virtually enslaved under convict leasing programs after the Civil War.

So instead of forbidding the institution itself, Islam forbade the inhumane treatment that was responsible for the injustice and continuance of that institution. This is the more humane solution given the reality on the ground in that time and place. The Qur'an and the Prophet attacked the slave mentality for both slave and master. Once slave and master were commanded that *"your slaves are your brethren"* and they were given time to have this teaching enforced by the Prophet and his Companions, slaves became enfranchised to seek their freedom, and masters became more conscious of their slaves' welfare. All the Companions freed their slaves before they died. It is a FACT that the second Caliph Umar Ibn Al-Khattab (12–22 AH) ordered all slaves in the empire to be freed. He is even quoted as saying, *"Do not enslave those whose mothers bore them free."* Also, the Caliph Umar Ibn Abdul-Aziz (95–98 AH) used funds from the public House of Money to feed all the hungry, house all the poor, help all singles get married, and free all the captives. After all these social needs were met, there was still money to go around such that there was no longer anyone left to accept this charity.

Islam closed all doors for people entering slavery except one: captured in war. The Qur'an and the Prophet commanded kindness to slaves and forbade abusing them. The Qur'an and the Prophet opened many doors for people to leave slavery. Add this all up, and you see that the number of new slaves would decrease, the condition of current slaves would improve, and the number of freed slaves would increase. Thus we see how Islam put in place rules that if followed religiously would lead to the disappearance of slavery without the turmoil of sudden abolishment.

As for your "maidservant from Asia" example, it would not be permissible to have sex with her without marriage between you and her. Sex would only be permissible after that contract is signed and witnessed. Even though you call her a "maidservant," **she is still a free woman,** so sex with her is not lawful without marriage. Islam allows a man to marry more than one wife so long as he can support each equally and impartially. If you can accept this, then it is easy to understand. If you do not accept this, then we have to back up our discussion to the issue of multiple wives.

As for how this is different from keeping a mistress, Islam defines adultery as sexual pleasure without responsibility. The man is responsible for the financial and material support of the woman and any children that result from the union. The woman is responsible for her loyalty and fidelity to the man.

Finally, as to how a slave girl fits into this discussion, remember that all the rules regarding slaves (including concubines) were revealed and developed in the *social context* of **an existing institution of slavery.** This institution no longer exists, so taking slaves or concubines is no longer allowed.

May peace be with you,
Ahmed

Email #26 – From: Kayan
Sent: Wednesday, February 29, 2012 10:31 a.m.

Dear Brother Rashed,

About adoption:

Most adopted children are an orphanage or from a natural calamity where they have lost their parents or from unwed mothers that don't want to raise the child. If I were such a child, I would rather have all the legal rights from my adoptive parents, rather than my birth parents that may not even be alive.

Verse 33:005 clearly says that adopted children should be called "brethren in faith." When I ask what is the harm in calling my adoptive son as my son rather than call him a brother in faith, you say this is to protect lineage but somehow justify breaking the same lineage rules when it comes to Adam and Eve's children having sex amongst themselves. Rules should be universal without exceptions — same rule for urbanite American as for Australian Aborigine and for Adam and his children. Guess it basically comes down to the universal question: is good simply because God commands it, even though our moral standards condemn the same act?

If you read ahead in the Qur'an, you will see that Prophet Muhammad wanted to marry his adopted son's wife, and after Zaid divorced her, Prophet Muhammad married her. Even in those medieval times, this was taboo, since adopted children were given the same rights as biological children, and Prophet Muhammad could not have married Zainab without first "getting a revelation" abolishing adoption as it stood in those times. Could this have been the reason for the adoption verse in the Qur'an?

About women's intelligence:

How does the Prophet know that those few women were ungrateful to their husbands? If they were stingy with their donations, how does that make them ungrateful to their husbands? Additionally, aren't all women disallowed from praying and fasting during their menses? Isn't the witness of ANY women equal to half that of a man?

About slavery:

Why do common people from captured lands have to be imprisoned as wards of the state or enslaved? When America captured Germany, Japan, Iraq, and Afghanistan, they did not enslave anyone, nor did they imprison the common people. They just let them be — why is that not a better option than either imprisoning them or enslaving them?

Regarding adultery:

By your logic, if my maidservant from Asia legally enters into a contract with me to work for me in return, for which I give her a place to stay, feed her, clothe her, and be responsible for her, what is required for me to share a bed with her? It cannot be marriage, since the slave masters did not marry their slaves.

You also said that the responsibilities of a slave master toward his female slave were similar to that of a husband towards his wife — I do not agree with that contention at all. Can a husband sell his wife? He can sell his slave, though (with the exception of one that he has children from).

Peace

Email #27 – From: Ahmed Rashed
Sent: Thursday, March 1, 2012 10:45 a.m.

Mr. Kayan:

You are arguing for the sake of argument. I already told you the Islamic stance on adoption and explained the true situation of Zaid. I already told you that even socially conservative scholars do not interpret that Hadith to denigrate women. I already told you why Islam did not outright abolish slavery. I already told you the definition of adultery in Islam; why concubines at the time of slavery's institution did not constitute adultery; and why with slavery's current abolishment, it is not permissible to take slaves or concubines.

Our job is only to convey the authentic teachings of Islam; it is not our job to convince you to accept Islam or its teachings.

The Qur'an says:

Had God so willed, He would indeed have given them all His guidance. (6:35)

Are the faithful unaware that, had He pleased, God could have guided all mankind? (13:31)

Yet had We so willed, We could indeed have imposed Our guidance upon every human being (32:13)

There will be both believers and disbelievers on this earth. This is part of God's Plan and Wisdom. So we already know that not everyone will accept this faith.

Even at the time of the Prophet, when there were miracles and signs proving that he was really sent by the Creator of the Universe, still many did not believe. People witnessed the splitting of the moon (Prophet Muhammad), the raising of the dead (Prophet Jesus), and the parting of the sea (Prophet Moses), and STILL there were eyewitnesses who refused to see the truth of these Prophets' message. It is understood that there will be some hearts that will simply not accept or be convinced of our claim to truth, no matter what is said.

May peace be with you,
Ahmed

Email #28 – From: Kayan
Sent: Friday, March 2, 2012 9:58 a.m.

Dear Brother Rashed,

Of course I understand that no one can convince me to accept or reject any faith system. Especially since Islam claims to be the ONLY TRUE religion, so I think I can reasonably expect all questions to be answered without a shadow of doubt. If I was discussing Buddhism or any other nonmonotheistic religion, that would not be the case. They don't claim that all other paths are wrong and that adherents of all other faiths are sinners.

But Islam clearly discriminates between Muslims and non-Muslims by calling all non-Muslims sinners; therefore, you have a greater burden of proving your contentions.

You say **"Had God so willed, He would indeed have given them all His guidance."** This means he has specifically chosen not to bring me or a majority of this world's population to guidance. Am I to conclude that he deliberately led us astray and is then promising us eternal punishment for something that HE chose for us? How is this indicative of a merciful and loving God?

Reason and logic are the cornerstone of human development. It is surprising to see people that demand reason and logic in every other sphere of their lives simply fold in to illogical fallacies when it comes to religion, so much so that they try to reinterpret 1,500-year-old scripture from a tribal culture to fit into today's moral landscape. This, especially in the case of the Qur'an, is akin to blasphemy due to the following verse: **And it becometh not a believing man or a believing woman, when Allah and His messenger have decided a matter, that they should have any say in that matter; and whoso is rebellious to Allah and His messenger, he verily goeth astray in error manifest. (33:36)**

The above verse effectively bans any attempt at reforming Islam. Thank you for your time.

Best regards and peace to you,
Kayan

Email #29 – From: Ahmed Rashed
Sent: Monday, March 5, 2012 10:36 a.m.

In the Name of God, Most Gracious, Most Merciful:
　　Faith springs from the heart, Kayan; and then it is confirmed by the mind … not the other way around.
　　May peace be with you,
　　Ahmed

With Dialogue Comes Understanding

THE
PHILOSOPHER
DIALOGUES

The Philosopher Dialogues

The Problem of Evil

Email #02 – From: David
Sent: Tuesday, July 21, 2015 1:30 p.m.

Hi Ahmed,

I teach religious studies, so I am familiar with Islam and especially its history. What I am curious about is new thinking in Islam. The biggest problem for any belief in Allah or God is the Problem of Evil. If we praise God for creation, then why do we not condemn God for causing so much suffering? If God is good, then why is there so much suffering? The modern world does not sustain the old defenses from the past; we know too much about how the world comes into being to believe old myths, and we know that we do not need a God for a moral universe. In fact, God only makes the universe less moral, because if we think of God as in control of creation, then God is the author of all this suffering.

Some will say the issue is the word "unjustified." How could we know what is justified from God's perspective? Fair enough, but that means that God is inexplicable and monstrous, because at any time incomprehensible suffering could be imposed on me with no reasonable explanation, from my point of view. On that account, God is random and malicious, not actually God. To claim that believing in God is good in this context is a moral absurdity; it is tantamount to worshiping chaos and misery.

Some will say the suffering is a consequence of decisions. But that does not explain the suffering caused by nature or in nature. It also fails utterly and completely once we notice that there is no good reason to believe that human beings actually make free decisions. Everything we know from science suggests free will is a useful illusion, so hardly a defense of a God who causes suffering. What does Islam, what do modern Muslims say about these issues?

Thanks,
David

Email #03 – From: Ahmed Rashed
Sent: Saturday, July 25, 2015 9:48 a.m.

In the Name of God, Most Gracious, Most Compassionate

Hi David,

These are very good points. However, in this particular issue (the Problem of Evil), modern Islamic philosophy has not diverged much from traditional Islamic philosophy.

The Problem of Evil is usually stated this way:

P1. An all-powerful God is able to prevent evil.

P2. An all-knowing God is aware of all evil in the world.

P3. An all-good God wants to prevent evil in the world.

P4. There is evil/suffering in the world.

C. Therefore, there is no God that is all-powerful, all-knowing, and all-good.

The crux of the argument is that the existence of evil in the world precludes at least one of these attributes of traditional God. The traditional Islamic response and what modern Islamic philosophers have not changed significantly is that there is a hidden assumption in this argument:

P0. The purpose of life is to live contented and blissfully.

Muslim philosophers to this day challenge this premise. They argue that this is the purpose of Heaven or Paradise, but not this worldly life. Rather, the Qur'an mentions in several places that this world is only a temporary proving ground, the sole purpose of which is to test the faith of mankind. Here are some samples of these verses for reference:

6:165 For it is Hewho has made you inherit the earth, and has raised some of you by degrees above others, so that He might try you by means of what He has bestowed upon you.

7:168 ... And the latter We tried with blessings as well as with afflictions, so that they might mend their ways.

18:7 We have willed that all beauty on earth be a means to put men to a test: which of them are best in conduct;

67:2 He who has created death as well as life, so that He might put you to a test: which of you is best in conduct ...

With this goal in mind, the conclusion above does not necessarily follow, because it is possible that there could exist a God who allows the evil we see and experience for the purpose of testing the faith of men. Muslim philosophers argue that if the purpose of life was to eat, drink, and be merry, then yes, the existence of evil and suffering would contradict the attributes of God. However, if we replace that assumption with the belief that this life is only a spiritual test, we can reconcile the existence of evil with the attributes of God.

Notice that this hinges on the belief in Judgment Day, the Final Reckoning, and Heaven/Hell. Since these are cardinal articles of faith for entire spectrum of Muslims (conservative to liberal), Muslim scholars have considered and continue to consider this a sufficient to answer the Problem of Evil.

Please pardon my long email and my delay in getting back to you. I look forward to continuing this discussion or opening another topic as you wish.

May peace be with you,
Ahmed

Email #04 – From: David
Sent: Saturday, July 25, 2015 1:43 p.m.

Hi Ahmed,

That is very sophisticated but not quite on target. You cannot use an appeal to a surface-level reading of the text to defend the text itself against the Problem of Evil. The Problem is a rational one and must be answered by reason. The text is part of what is being questioned in the Problem itself. Other than the text itself, what evidence do you have for this divine plan? Well, none. That is why this Problem haunts every type of theism.

What you have stumbled into (although you phrased it very well) is just circular reasoning. How do I know that Allah has this plan? The text says so. How do I know the text is reliable? The text says so. Circle.

The problem that reason has is that when we look at the totally unjustified suffering in the world, we discover that in many cases we cannot even imagine any further action or creation (any heaven) that could compensate for the suffering.

I have a radical thought. What if Allah is not a word that picks out a being, divine being, or even the source of being, but rather Allah is the name we give to a feeling we have, a feeling we associate with spirituality or mystical practice. God is not the source of our religious feelings; rather, God is the name of those feelings.

What I am suggesting is that the divine is not a category of being (not ontology) but rather a category of experience (epistemology). We, human beings, have long thought of the divine as a being outside of us, and then often as a being that is part of us; but I am moving past that to say what is real is the feeling, and we were just mistaken to focus so much attention on the source. We need to realize that what is of value is the religious experience, not the supposed source of it.

More personally, the whole notion of life as a test seems odd to me. Why would a divine being want to create any context in which its creatures would suffer so tremendously, many of them totally innocent? Is it to test some of them? God cannot be testing the newborn babies who die horribly from starvation. But their suffering is part of that test, but part of someone else's test? You see, this is not a moral act. This is not how moral beings behave — they do not use the suffering of innocent beings for purposes beyond them. The god you describe does not seem like a moral being to me, but not just you, of course; this is true of all traditional theism. It describes a god that is actually quite arbitrary and monstrous. Do you understand that criticism? It is the deepest one, of course. And I think my appeal to experience solves the problem.

Let me know what you think.

Yours,

David

Email #05 – From: Ahmed Rashed
Sent: Wednesday, July 29, 2015 11:06 a.m.

In the Name of God, Most Gracious, Most Compassionate

Hi David,

Let us step back for a moment. This is an academic discussion, not a confessional one. The purpose was not to convince you, but rather to convey the philosophy and understanding that Muslim scholars have had and continue to have on the subject with the understanding that this information will be used by you to accurately represent the Islamic response to the Problem of Evil in your religious studies class.

As I mentioned in the previous email, the entire Muslim response to the Problem of Evil hinges on acceptance on one axiom: the existence of a Day of Judgment and subsequent hereafter. As an axiom, this is the premise that must be accepted without external proof to support the rest of the argument.

You are correct that this problem haunts all forms of theism, including Islam. However, my purpose is not to convince you that the Problem of Evil is not a problem, but rather to simply convey how Muslim scholars to this day respond to it. If a person accepts the axiom of hereafter, as most Muslim scholars do, then the "Life is a Test" response is satisfactory. What proof is there that this axiom is actually true? As you said, the text itself, so the response is circular. I concede that; but remember that most Muslim scholars already accept the axioms of Islamic faith (belief in God, Angels, Prophets, Scriptures, hereafter, and Divine Decree), so it is not a problem for Muslims. If the problem of evil is the reason why someone would reject theism, then that person would require something beyond and outside of these axioms as a starting point. However, if a person starts with those axioms already internalized, then the Problem of Evil is nothing more than a doubt or crisis of faith, whereby the explanation I've given you is enough to assuage that doubt.

As an undergrad, I did a research paper on the Problem of Evil, and in that paper I put forward arguments similar to what I had discussed in my previous email. In addition, I challenged the definition of benevolence that traditional critics of theism used to dismiss the "Life is a Test" response. I don't have the details of that paper with me anymore, so forgive me if this reply seems light on proper exposition. The gist of that paper was how can any human being encompass what is "too much suffering" or "enough suffering" or "inappropriate suffering" or "appropriate suffering?" Without an alternative existence, how can one see that there was a different set of suffering that is less than what we observed but would satisfy the requirement of testing and spiritual development? By what standard would we judge God? You see, it is simply replacing one set of assumptions with another equally arbitrary set of assumptions.

On the other hand, the "Life is a Test" response explicitly predicts that life will include circumstances that will test a person's faith, that will make someone doubt the existence and benevolence of God, and that will leave one to wonder where God is in all this. If life's suffering was NOT of this level, then faith would not be tested, and that would defeat the purpose of Life to begin with … is this circular? If I have a mining operation, and I extract iron ore from the ground, and I put that ore through a refining process to extract the pure iron from the dross, how does the iron judge (figuratively speaking) that I am applying "enough heat" or "inappropriately excessive heat" to it? If the whole purpose of the refining process is to apply heat and pressure so the components of the ore can be separated into its different qualities of material (high-purity iron, low-purity iron, rock, and dross), then the refining process is "appropriate" and "justified" to fulfill the higher purpose of refining.

You might respond that the moral justification for such a context still has not been addressed … why would God do this to His creation? The Islamic answer takes us to a different branch of Islamic philosophy, so I'll stop here for your reply and then we can continue this discussion, God-willing.

May peace be with you,
Ahmed

The Philosopher Dialogues

The Question of Euthyphro

Email #06 – From: David
Sent: Thursday, July 30, 2015 2:37 p.m.

Hi Ahmed,

I appreciate the seriousness with which you take my questions. And you are right that it all comes down to your final paragraph. "Why would God do this to God's creation?"

In one of his dialogues (the Euthyphro) Plato takes up this question and ends with a surprising conclusion. If God is understandable to us, then God is not needed by us because we can reason our way to anything God would tell us. If God is not understandable, then God is simply a brutal dictator imposing suffering for no apparent reason, and hardly an object of worship. That God is merely demanding conformity out of fear, not respect — hardly a divine move. I think this is the answer to the question you raised in that paper. We are the ones to judge, because we are the ones worshipping. If God is not rationally defensible as an object of worship, then the religion becomes a morass of irrationality. Some critics would say this is the point, but our conversation assumes some value to religion beyond that.

The first problem is bad enough — why do we need God if we have reason — but the second — the one you have picked up — makes things even worse. How can anyone relate to a God who is inexplicably cruel? On another note, what is this different branch of philosophy you had in mind?

Yours,
David

Email #07 – From: Ahmed Rashed
Sent: Saturday, August 1, 2015 1:38 p.m.

In the Name of God, Most Gracious, Most Compassionate

Hi David,

I also appreciate your respect in engaging this dialogue. I will get to the final paragraph in a moment, but first I'd like to talk about Euthyphro first:

My understanding of the question of Euthyphro is:

1) Is good called "good" because God said it is good?

or

2) Does God say that good is "good" because it is good?

The argument is:

If you select number 1, then "good" really has no meaning. It is strictly dependent upon God's will. So if God said that raping an innocent child was good, then that is "good." So "good" on this view is arbitrary and not objective.

If you select number 2, then "good" is a standard independent of God. But isn't God the source of all things?

The Islamic rebuttal is actually based on the Jewish philosophers' response to this:

Our moral values and duties are determined by God's commands, but these commands are not arbitrary, because they are expressions of the very nature of God Himself, which is immutable, necessary, noncontingent and ultimately GOOD. God Himself is the standard, and His commands are expressions of His Essence, which by definition is immutable.

In order for Judgment and Reckoning to have any meaning, there must be some absolute standard that is independent of popular opinion. Islam says that Absolute Standard is God, since He is The Truth and The Source of Goodness and The Guide. The story of Euthyphro itself at the end hints that there must be an objective standard called "The Good," and this "The Good" must be good in and of itself out of necessity and not arbitrarily, and it also must be the standard itself (i.e., the standard must not exist independently)

However, no philosopher is free of the cultural context that he lives in. That is a subtle point that must be recognized. Since Plato was living in a polytheistic era where "the gods" were fighting one another and had petty personalities, he concluded that Selecting #1 meant the capricious whims of one or many "gods" automatically become "good," which of course is distasteful to him and most people who think of this question.

It was the Jewish philosophers who identified this implied premise. The Jews responded that "The Good" that was being spoken about was actually the One God Himself, since He by definition is "The Good." Muslims also believe this, since one of Allah's names is Al Barr.

Tangentially, all of these theological/philosophical problems are solved by referring to the Beautiful Names of God and realizing that God is ONE with these Names/Attributes. See this link for more detailed explanations of each:

http://wahiduddin.net/words/wazifa.htm

Anyway, this is why the classical scholars define *tawheed* (monotheism) as having three branches: believing that God is one in His Lordship (creation, resurrection, judgment, etc.), that God is one in His Divinity (right to be worshiped, praised, and glorified), and that God is one in His Names/Attributes. That last part means that if you deny or leave out any one of these attributes, you have misrepresented God and fallen into a type of polytheism.

Trying to tie up all these points, the issue is not so much whether God is understandable or not. Rather, the issue is whether God, being beyond our full, comprehensive understanding (as Islam firmly states) can still be an objective and Ultimate Source of Truth, Good, Beauty, and so on. Islam teaches that full understanding, fully comprehending God, is not possible, but we can glean glimpses of His Wisdom, Benevolence, and Power by applying our reasoning and observations. The issue is not black or white, as Plato wrote. It is not explicable vs. inexplicable ... there are levels of understanding that we CAN achieve, and there are levels that we cannot, so Plato's binary either/or conclusion is missing a third middle ground. The only leap of faith to make, as I said in the first email, is whether we are willing to trust that God is a benevolent creator ... that is the test of faith; if not, we conclude He is nonexistent or at best ambivalent and useless.

This brings us to the end of my last email: Why would God create the world in this way?

When people ask "What is the Purpose of Life," the Muslim philosopher responds that these are actually three different questions, which have three different answers:

The "Operational" Purpose of Life — Why am I here? What am I expected to do in life?

The "Existential" Purpose of Life — Why does this world exist? What is it expected to be?

The "Transcendental" Purpose of Life — Why did God create?

The answer to #1 is clearly stated in the Qur'an: "To worship God." However the Arabic word *'ibadah* does not mean only worship. Rather it has nuances of seeking, finding, and devotion. So scholars have summed it up: the purpose of Man in this life is "to Seek God, and from Seeking God, to Know God, and from Knowing God, to Love God, and from Loving God, to Honor and Worship God." This is the nature of the relationship that Man is expected to have regarding God.

The answer to #2 is also clearly stated in the Qur'an: "To test Man who is best in deeds." This is what we started our discussion with when we addressed the Problem of Evil from the Islamic perspective.

The answer to #3 is from the discussions of the scholars, especially Ibn Arabi and Ibn Taymiyya. They concluded from the Qur'anic verses about God's attributes and names and from the Prophet's Sayings about seeking and loving God that "Knowing God" is the reason why God created. In other words, God wished to create beings that could Know Him and created a world where that knowing could be developed.

The angels, being without free will, could not "know" all

of God's names, since they could not experience wrath, or forgiveness, or grace, etc. It is important in Islamic theology to emphasize God's choice in creation. Some other traditions use God's name, "The Creator," to imply that creation was a necessary consequence; however, Islam rejects this because then there would be something "above" God's will. God is the ultimate reality, and His will is the ultimate first cause that is contingent on nothing but Himself. So a dangerous world filled with natural disasters and death and populated by free willing human beings who could do good or evil was created for the purpose of making God manifest and known in all His names.

Just a quick clarification about knowing God vs. understanding God: the Arabic language has two words for "knowing": *'alamah* and *'arafah*. The first word is used for objective knowledge and is where we get God's name, the All-Knowing (*Al-'Aleem*). The second word is used for subjective knowledge, specifically knowledge that was initially absent but then later acquired. This is where we get the word *"Ma'rifah,"* which is what Ibn Taymiyya called the Transcendental Purpose of Life: *"Ma'rifah Allah,"* the implication of this word, and Ibn Taymiyya's work is that God created Man and this world so that Man could go from Ignorance of God to Knowing (*'arafah*) God, realizing that it is impossible to perfectly Understand (*'alamah*) God.

May peace be with you,
Ahmed

Email #08 – From: David
Sent: Saturday, August 1, 2015 5:32 p.m.

Hi Ahmed,

I have never actually seen the full 99 list in English (and I don't read Arabic). Thanks!

I can't fault your tenacity or background knowledge. You are very smart and good with arguments.

By *Good*, Plato meant the *Form of The Good*, which he regarded as the highest Form, the one that gave reality to the others. It is a later religious reading (actually from the Neo-Platonists) that first read Good as God.

What I think I have come to is that the real challenge in the Euthyphro is that we cannot help but be the judge. Is the Good good because God said so? That is does God define good? That implies that reason cannot understand the good alone. Thus, God is arbitrary to reason. Or is the Good good because reason tells us and God agrees (confirms)? That implies that reason does not need God. Thus, God is unnecessary. God is unnecessary or incomprehensible (but also beyond any relationship)?

So we cannot escape our reason. The appeal of theism is not to reason but to authority. The problem is the authority has no way to validate itself except by reason, because we cannot help but treat reason as the judge of these sorts of things (that is what I am saying is the lesson of the Euthyphro). Reason finds god, understood ontologically, unnecessary or incomprehensible.

The texts don't help because their authority depends on this larger question. So what is reason to do? I think this is where the Enlightenment theology gets stuck.

You naturally frame God as being a question of ontology: God must exist or not. I think that is the Enlightenment holding on to a past it did not question (a commitment to ontology in religion). I suggested the better frame is knowledge — epistemology. But that demands a very different theology, although one that could be perfectly comfortable in Islam or the other theisms.

Back to the 99 names, my take on that is the reason there are so many is because our human experience of feeling connected to others, and a larger natural reality comes in many forms. Religious experiences have many varieties (*à la* William James), but what is really real is not a being at the other end of the feeling (a cause); rather, what is really real is the feeling (the religious experience, or spirituality, but fundamentally a feeling of being connected or related.

I am actually writing a book of theology based on that idea. If you are curious, I could send you some working notes.

Reason does not sustain the claim of theism, I am suggesting. But experience tells us religion is important. How do we reconcile this? My suggestion is that it is through a reconstruction of the core symbol, God. Thus, God is not a being or even Being, but the name for a particular sort of feeling that is common to humans, a feeling of connection of various sorts. The various traditions are important because they are the enduring social core of the religion and could be infused with this sort of worldview, rather than a theistic one, and still be Islam or Judaism or whatever.

Is there any philosopher in the Islamic world who talks like this? And do you get my point about reason demands a different answer?

In Jewish and Christian thought, some work has been done coming to terms with human authorship of the texts. The textual scholars have convinced anyone open to reason that the texts, Hebrew TANAK and Christian Bible, are the work of multiple human authors and editors acting over long periods of time, and that most of the texts had their origins in oral traditions that extended for decades or centuries past the events behind them. In Islam the issues are very different, but Islam cannot avoid the information that the Jewish and Christian sources are of human origin. Are there any Islamic scholars, philosophy or theology types, who talk about these sorts of things?

Salam,
David

Email #09 – From: Ahmed Rashed
Sent: Monday, August 10, 2015 11:03 a.m.

In the Name of God, Most Gracious, Most Compassionate

Hi David,

You are welcome for the 99 names link.

The Form of Good vs. the Nature of God; yes, this is precisely the conundrum. Most Muslim scholars would state that God defines good.

So in one sense, good is arbitrary *vis à vis* reason. However, the appeal to God's 99 names tries to assuage that arbitrariness by claiming that part of believing in God is also believing that God ultimately cares about our well-being and there is a benevolent reason behind all that He does.

This is an axiom of faith, I admit; but that is what the majority of Muslim scholars argue.

Interestingly, Islamic thought has a heritage of elevating human reason and arguing that faith is very compatible with reason. In fact, the Mu'tazilites were trail-blazers in that area of arguing that reason alone could be used to find God based on their understanding of (2:163-164):

Your God is one God. There is no god but He, the Benevolent, the Compassionate. In the creation of the heavens and the earth; in the alternation of night and day; in the ships that sail the oceans for the benefit of mankind; in the water that God sends down from the sky, and revives the earth with it after it had died, and scatters in it all kinds of creatures; in the changing of the winds, and the clouds subdued between the sky and the earth; are signs for people who try to understand.

So they argue that even without the "signs" of revealed scriptures, the "signs" of the natural world are sufficient for a subgroup of people, "those who try to understand." The Arabic is particular in that last verse; it is a derivative of the word that means to restrain emotion and think objectively. Also, the word is used in the infinitive sense, not present or past, so it is incorrect to translate as "people who understand" or "people who attained understanding," so the Mu'tazilites point out that the continual effort of seeking God and understanding God is a way or path to finding, appreciating, and loving God. The Mu'tazilites fell out of popularity back in the seventeenth century as Muslim culture began declining intellectually. A few modern scholars have Mu'tazilite leanings, for example Egyptian theologian Muhammad Ghazali and Turkish mystic Bediuzzaman Sa'id Nursi.

Even for these scholars, the "personality" of God is important. The idea that what is really real at the end of these feelings and thoughts is a human experience rather than a Divine Being would be challenged, I think. Fundamentally, this is the new axis of philosophical discussion about the question of God and Theism. However, Islam as a religion places the Being of God, the Mind and Will of God, very prominently, so I am not sure a "social core" would be sufficient for Islam.

I would be interested to see some of your working notes on that book you mentioned. Looking forward to continuing the discussion!

May peace be with you,
Ahmed

An Alternative Theology of God

Email #10 – From: David
Sent: Wednesday, August 12, 2015 1:54 p.m.

Hi Ahmed,

I attached my draft, just working notes really. What I haven't mentioned yet is that I am Jewish (my PhD-level education was Christian, though). I therefore situate my thoughts in that tradition, but what I hope people will see in what I am doing is that this move is open to any religion.

It might be that Christianity, especially in the Western world, and Judaism, also especially in the Western world, both embraced the Enlightenment. Conservative trends in both reject it, and I think Islam is in that position today. Islam has not embraced the Enlightenment yet.

In comparative religion, the other idea that has some traction is that Islam never had a reformation. Judaism had its only in the 1800s. Islam has not yet had that rush at modernizing. Many people would blame the Wahhabi influence since the elevation of the House of Saud. The other schools of thought might have done more if they had more freedom of action.

What do you think of all that? The challenge to divine being as central is something that goes back at least a century now in Christian theology and has been prominent for at least sixty years. Jewish theology is slower to move in that direction (my work is a radical jump in that regard). It sounds like that idea hasn't made any inroads in Islam yet. I predict it will.

(Editor's note: The draft essay was over twenty pages long and very theologically heavy. Below are the relevant excerpts for this discussion.)

> The title of this essay comes from a biblical story, Numbers 16. In that story, Korach and some 250 followers challenge Moses' and Aaron's authority and are annihilated. The story is usually interpreted as being about the importance of accepting divine

authority, and with it priestly authority. But there is another reading, not just hinted at but demanded by the text. Korach does not say that he wants authority. What he wants is for all the Hebrews to have access to the divine, not just the priests. He is challenging the whole structure of priestly authority, not just selfishly asking for it himself.

* * *

The view I am trying to articulate sees God as more like a sunset than a spirit or person. Everything we know we know from our experience. Everything known is fundamentally an experience to us. What lies behind the experience can be vexing at times. At other times it is pretty easy, like the cat purring on my lap. But what is a sunset? It is not a thing. Ontology is really the wrong territory to talk about it unless all we want to know is about dust and reflection. All of that science does not tell us about the beauty of the sunset. The beauty is our response to a particular visual experience. It is not mysterious to science but is to poetry because the magnitude of how we respond to beauty is mysterious to us. The value of the sunset does not depend on my analysis of it. It is intrinsic in some sense in the experience. I am saying that God is like that. What we call God is a myriad of interacting causes that produce an experience. We value the experience, and because we really like understanding things, we suppose that there is a cause to know. That is the mistake. The value in the experience called God, the religious experience, is not its cause but its effect. The value in all of it is the feeling itself. The feeling is what we call God. God is not the source or cause of the feeling, but rather the name we give to certain, profound sorts of experiences.

* * *

The problem is this commitment to ontology, to being. What if God is not about Being or even my being, but about a connection with reality, nature, and/or people that is deeply felt and deeply important? What we call God, I believe, is not a being or even Being, but the feeling of connection at the heart of religious experience. God is not the source or cause of that feeling, God is the name of the feeling. Does God exist? Of course. Many people report that feeling. God is not the source of that feeling. God is the feeling itself. And always has been. We were just confused about how to relate to this feeling that is so powerful and seemingly vitally important. The feeling must have a cause, and so we assumed what we call God caused it. But there is no God in that sense. God is the feeling. That special feeling of connecting to reality, to nature, to another is God. It is good and important, vital to the human experience and history. God is what moves history. God the feeling is also the feeling of righteous indignation, which does move history. God is not a metaphysical term about ontology, but rather God is an epistemological term about how we experience and know reality.

* * *

Salam,
David

Email #11 – From: Ahmed Rashed
Sent: Thursday, August 27, 2015 11:01 a.m.

In the Name of God, Most Gracious, Most Compassionate

Hi David,

Wow; that was a very deep read. There are some aspects that I agree with, for example, the idea of "experiencing God" because it is similar to the "knowing God" arguments put forward by Ibn Taymiyya. However, as I mentioned before, the Person of God as an actual being is very central to Islam and to the teachings of the Prophet, so this transformation of the concept of God is not something that most Muslims would accept. On the other hand, you are correct that there has not yet been a "Muslim Reformation" or "Enlightenment" … we are only in the Islamic Year 1436, so we Muslims are due for one sometime this century!

The interesting question is whether Islamic philosophy and theology can ever go in the direction that Christian or Jewish theology went. See, there is a textual gap in Judaism and Christianity that makes it possible to view those scriptures as products of human agency and interpretation. Such leeway is only possible because the original sayings and teachings from the prophets themselves are not available. However, Islam has "too much documentation" for that to be tenable. The Qur'an was recited multiple times each year until Prophet Muhammad died. When the first manuscript was compiled, it was NOT a rewriting of people's memories; rather, it was a gathering of those words that were written under the direct supervision of the Prophet into one leather folder. That collection was crosschecked against the memories of a half-dozen Companions who had memorized the Qur'an entirely from the Prophet himself. Ever since then, all Qur'ans have been copies of that original collection.

So in a sense, an orthodox Muslim cannot but accept that the Qur'an we have now is the exact same Qur'an that Prophet Muhammad taught in seventh century Arabia and that the Companions learned and lived by. Therefore, a person can argue whether the Qur'an is really from God or just some figment of Muhammad's imagination, but if that person accepts the Qur'an as God's Word, then he could not do away with the explicit descriptions of God's attributes as having a will, a sense of being, and a sense of "personality." The texts preclude the concept of God as *"a myriad of interacting causes that produce an experience,"* as you explain in the essay.

The Prophet explicitly described to his Companions what he felt and saw and heard when Revelation descended upon him. So unless Muhammad was crazy or lying, it is difficult for those who believe that Muhammad was true to interpret God as "the effect of religious experience" rather than the traditional "cause of religious experience." I appreciate the motive behind the transition from "God up there" to "God as experience." However, it is not the only solution to the Problem of Evil.

As for free will, it is interesting that you argue (or seem to argue) that evidence points to free will as an illusion, which is a statement most Muslims would strongly disagree with. However, near the end of that section, you say something that all Muslims would strongly agree with: "But in truth a person cannot be evil, they can only do evil. Their being cannot be counter to human flourishing, but their behavior certainly can."

May peace be with you,
Ahmed

The Philosopher Dialogues

A Muslim Reformation?
Email #12 – From: David
Sent: Saturday, August 29, 2015 1:46 p.m.

Hello Ahmed,

What is most fun for me about this conversation is that you know your history and can tell me about someone like Taymiyya. I know there are four major schools of thought, but I could not name them and certainly do not know the major figures in them. I am learning a lot this way. This is the part that I hoped would help me as a teacher.

The rest is me as a writer. I appreciate your taking the time to read it and comment. I am putting forth a view that will not be accepted by traditional theists, but my audience is really people who have left religion but still feel like they are missing something. Those people might respond.

More significant and related to learning about Islam, I am still curious about this reformation question. In modern theology it is true that human authorship is a big deal, but the reformation itself assumed the traditional view of God. Now, what may be structurally different is that Islam does not have priests, and so a challenge to that office is not possible. What would an Islamic reformation look like? Judaism might be a model because it doesn't have priesthood any more. And did not during its Reformation. But the problem may be that by the time of that Reformation, most Jews already had moved away from traditional theism. Not all, though, so there is overlap in views to be found.

Christianity fought the priesthood; Judaism fought a traditional way of life that was out of place. For Islam to have a reformation, it would have to have some focus that was critical of its past and saw a way forward from that criticism. Maybe it is not part of the history because Islam did not do the things that motivated those challenges in the other religions?

Maybe the model is Jewish, and Islam will reform by adapting new ways of thinking about Sharia. The problem that

ultraorthodox Judaism has is that it does not fit the modern world. If everyone behaved like them, the world economy would stop functioning. Most of Judaism behaves in a more modern way. Is this true about Islam to some degree? The traditional life as described textually is simply different from and out of place in the world we now inhabit (modern technology, world integration, and global capitalism). If everyone behaved like Islamic traditionalists, the global economy would collapse, like the issue with very conservative forms of Judaism. It is that life that Reform Judaism rejected. Is there a model in there for Islam, a way to blend religious life and modern lifestyles that looks like a reformation because the change is dramatic? Thanks again!
Salam,
David

Email #13 – From: Ahmed Rashed
Sent: Thursday, September 3, 2015 11:37 a.m.

In the Name of God, Most Gracious, Most Compassionate
Hello David,
So an Islamic Reformation would look like a recontextualization of the source texts (Qur'an and Prophetic Sayings). Right now, even "liberal" Muslim scholars stay rather close to the top-level meaning of those texts. Only if the text itself is ambiguous or conditional would they even consider delving into more metaphorical or ancillary meanings.

Remember, at its heart, Islam is not about orthodoxy vs. heterodoxy; it is about orthopraxy. That means that there is practically no significant difference in creed or belief, because the texts are so clear and explicit. However, Islamic practice and norms are not couched in such explicit terminology.

So there would never be a debate on whether murder, adultery, and stealing are sinful and criminal acts.

However, the punishment for those convicted of these crimes (which currently ARE talked about in Qur'an and Sayings) would have to be recontextualized in a Reformation attempt. Of course, this is only if Muslims decided and accepted to practice these teachings in a different manner than what historical precedence would normally allow.

May peace be with you,
Ahmed

Email #14 – From: David
Sent: Thursday, September 3, 2015 1:48 p.m.

Hi Ahmed,

Perhaps you even know what some of this already looks like. Judaism is also orthopraxic, really even more than Islam, because Islam has a creed and Judaism does not. But Islam has made some accommodation of modern banking. Perhaps the model is like that. What were or are the conversations like about those sorts of issues inside Islam?

The texts accept slavery as a given, but we reject that as completely unacceptable in the modern world. The texts advocate the death penalty for mixing cotton and wool. We do not put people to death for mixing fabrics.

We ignore some of the things that are simply out of touch with our world, and we rethink other things that are important moral issues but in new ways.

What I think strikes most Westerners as most unrealistic about how they see Islam is the way you phrased this allegiance to the text. The twenty-first century is not the seventh, and the ways of life in each are different. To think that a moral text from 1,300 years ago would be completely informative today simply makes no sense. We have to think about a world with an Internet and drone warfare. We can be inspired by the past and our texts, but no modern person thinks we can simply live their life. I assume you do too — you use the Internet and other features of the modern world, like banks.

What we call Reformation in the other traditions is a reworking of the relationship between the present and the text. I think it is safe to say that it actually is happening in a disorganized way inside Islam, because Muslims everywhere have to figure out how they will life in the modern world.

I suspect there are people writing about these issues — it is just that they may be thought of as secular thinkers rather than religious because of how they are prioritizing their sources. Does that make any sense?

David

Email #15 – From: Ahmed Rashed
Sent: Monday, September 14, 2015 11:57 a.m.

In the Name of God, Most Gracious, Most Compassionate

Hi David,

Sorry for the extended delay. Work was crazy last week, and my mother had a wrist operation, so I did not have as much free time as usual.

There is a glimpse of what a reform in Islam would look like. Check out *Progressive Muslims: On Justice, Gender, and Pluralism*, edited by Omid Safi. It is a few years old, but it is still relevant as a primer on what progressive Muslim thinkers are going toward. Also, any book by Khaled Abou El Fadl would be good for you to read.

Allegiance to the text is what makes Islam what it is; the whole point (or premise) is that after all the man-made errors that crept into previous scriptures, there is finally revealed a Final Testament that sets the record straight and can be used as a universal guide for all people for all time. That is the whole hope of Islam as a theology. The text of the Qur'an is such that it CAN be used this way, since most of the verses are moral and general, with only a few that are specific and concrete. Even those are contextual, hence the reason I gave the examples I did in the previous email.

May peace be with you,
Ahmed

Email #16 – From: David
Sent: Tuesday, September 15, 2015 1:37 p.m.

Hi Ahmed,

I hope the surgery went well. Hands and wrists are so important to navigating the world; it would hard to not have use even for a short time.

I feel that we have arrived at an ending point here, but I don't want that ending. So I would like to leave you with some "elderly" advice...

In our conversation, you talk as if everything is determined and there are no differences. You need to let people know about Islam's variety, both in place and time. Much of what is Islamic practice is culturally bound. I know you are trying to teach people about the basic religion and its teaching, but you have to let them know there is a whole universe of cultural variety that is Islam too.

It is all so cold and formulaic. I am reminded here that you are an engineer. I read a great book by Abou El Fadl (I gather he is the most important Islamic scholar living in the west today), and he is worried that too many Western Muslim leaders (people stepping up to do things like you) are not trained in law, but in some technical science field. You all do not know philosophy or theology, and so your thinking about the complexities of religion are formulaic, not fluid.

As a lawyer, he is an expert in how Islam has changed. From your presentation, one might think nothing ever changes. But this is not only untrue but unhelpful. I mean this in a friendly way, as I started my academic life in an engineering college. It is not your fault you think like an engineer; you were taught to do that for good reasons. I know that as a philosopher and theologian, my training is very different. We ask questions engineers would not think could be asked.

From a theological angle, I would say you need to acknowledge that there is struggle with truth. We worry and wonder. Did we get it right?

The words you use are accurate in a cold, analytic way, but the tradition is also about life. Show people the life lived behind the words.

Anyway, that's enough from me! Farewell for now. Should I think of anything else to talk about, I will be in touch. For me this is the New Year, so *L'Shana Tova*! May you have a healthy and happy 5776 (on our calendar)!

Yours sincerely,
David

Email #17 – From: Ahmed Rashed
Sent: Thursday, September 17, 2015 9:04 a.m.

In the Name of God, Most Gracious, Most Compassionate
Hi David,

First of all, thank you for your concern. My mom is doing okay now, but she is still complaining of the pain. She has a follow-up next week so the doctor can monitor progress.

Secondly, thank you for your candid feedback. I truly appreciate it. I have also read Abou Fadl, and I agree with both of you that we need more diversity in the Muslim American volunteer community. Humanities majors are not as represented as technical majors. God-willing, I will talk to my community organizers and point out that we need to attract volunteers from all walks of life.

Finally, Happy New Year to you, too; may you have health and happiness. I agree that our conversation has wound down. I will keep in touch, God-willing, and look forward to more conversations.

May peace be with you,
Ahmed

The Philosopher Dialogues

With Dialogue Comes Understanding

WHY ISLAM?

Why Islam?

Islamic Theology and History

Email #02 – From: Rene
Sent: Saturday, March 4, 2017 4:24 a.m.

Hello Mr. Rashed:

Thank you for your email, as well as the information provided. I have several questions that I hope you will be able to answer. Thank you in advance for any answers you may provide.

In some places within the Qur'an, it is stated that righteous Jews, Christians, Sabians, and Muslims (i.e., anyone who believes in the one true God, rather than polytheism, atheism, etc.) will see Paradise. Yet another place contradicts this, stating that only those who believe in the final revelation, i.e., Islam, will be saved. Is there an official position on this?

How does Islam explain the crucifixion of Jesus? I have read several different answers to this question, which is why I pose it here. I have heard some say that it never happened to begin with; others say that someone resembling Jesus was crucified; some claim that he was crucified, did not die, but rather fainted; others still suggest that the crucifixion witnessed by the Jews who had him sentenced to death was a mass hallucination and did not really happen at all.

Some have told me that listening to music (other than nasheeds) is haram. Is this true? Obviously this would be the case for songs containing crude, profane, or suggestive/offensive lyrics, but what of those with completely innocent lyrics, or songs that are instrumental only?

Do the references to jihad in the Qur'an only refer to spiritual warfare or literal but self-defensive warfare? There are passages alluding to ambushing polytheists (please correct me if I'm wrong), which is not indicative of self-defense.

What is the Islamic position on abortion? Or do views tend to differ in this area?

Does the Qur'an really condone a man striking his wife in Surah 4:34? I find it difficult to reconcile this concept with what I have been told a woman's position is within Islam. My understanding is that women, especially mothers, are elevated to a higher status. This does not seem to be in harmony with this particular verse.

I have read that the Qur'an permits men to sleep with female captives of war as well as slaves. I am beginning to read the Qur'an in English, but I am by no means an expert, so please correct me if I am wrong on this.

I have heard Islam referred to as the "religion of peace" by Muslims. I understand that Islam's teachings, as well as much of the Qur'an, promotes peace, social justice, etc. — yet Islam was spread through wars, occupations, conquests of nations and kingdoms, etc. I don't understand how it can be claimed that it is peaceful when it was spread through such violent means.

I have read that apostasy in Islam is punishable by death in some Muslim-majority countries, despite the Qur'anic verse, "Let there be no compulsion in religion. Truth stands out clear from error." Surely there are no verses or Hadiths condoning this?

I was raised as a devout nondenominational Christian by a Church of Christ father and grandmother and a lapsed Roman Catholic mother. Religion has always played a very important role in my life, as has God and truth. Several years ago, I began studying my own religion closely, as well as others — I am fascinated by religion, culture, and religious history.

As someone who has studied the Bible as well as various Christian doctrines, I found inconsistencies in doctrine, tradition, and within the Bible itself. About a year ago, during a very dark time in my life (and what is sometimes called a night of faith), when I was doubting Christianity more than ever but did not refute that there is a God, several of my friends who are Muslims began gently urging me to consider Islam. They taught me about the religion and suggested I read the Qur'an.

Now, until they began to teach me about their beliefs, I knew only what has been propagated in the media: news stories and articles about the abhorrent actions of extremists. It was only when they shared their beliefs with me that I was able to see differently. After much studying, prayer, discussion, learning, etc., I am in a place where I will accept Islam if I can find answers to my questions, which I have related above.

Thank you for any answers as well as for your time. I appreciate it very much.
Sincerely,
Rene

Email #03 – From: Ahmed Rashed
Sent: Tuesday, March 7, 2017 2:09 p.m.

In the Name of God, Most Gracious, Most Compassionate
Hello Rene,

Seeking answers is always a painful process. May God make your journey easy, *ameen*. Here are my thoughts on your questions:

1. The official line was best explained by Imam Al-Ghazali, the famous twelfth century scholar and mystic. Dr. Sherman Jackson is a well-known Muslim scholar at the University of California. He translated many classical books and is well respected in the field. In his introduction to Imam Al-Ghazali's famous book *Theological Tolerance*, Dr. Jackson explains this issue as follows:

Al-Ghazali goes on, however, to insist that God's mercy will encompass non-Muslims as well, including "most of the Christians of Byzantium and the [non-Muslim] Turks of the age." These people he divides into three categories: 1) those who never heard so much as the name Muhammad; 2) those who heard his name and had access to concrete and authentic information about his life and mission; 3) those who heard of him but received wrong, insufficient, or misleading information about this life and mission. According to al-Ghazali, it is only those of the second category, who came into reliable and concrete information about Muhammad, and, in a spirit of defiance, persist in rejecting his Prophethood, who will dwell forever in Hellfire. This is because only such people can be said to be guilty of deeming the Prophet to be a liar. As for those of the first and third categories, these will be covered by God's all-encompassing mercy. For, ultimately, their nonacceptance of Muhammad's Prophethood is free of defiance and attributable to circumstances beyond their control.

This is the condition for eternal hellfire. Those who don't meet this condition will serve their time in Hell; but after that time, by God's mercy they may or may not be admitted to Paradise. In these cases, only God knows their final destination.

So both views are correct. When the Qur'an says that the only acceptable religion is "Islam," it is referring to the people who actually met the Prophet Muhammad during his lifetime or who received accurate, comprehensive information about the Prophet's message (the second category mentioned above). We know this because the occasion of this revelation was when the Prophet was debating with a delegation of Christian priests near the end of his life. However, when the Qur'an says that previous believers (Jews, Christians, Sabians, etc.) will have their reward, it is referring to people who never met the Prophet either due to time or distance. We know this because the occasion of this revelation was when the Prophet's Companion, Salman, worried that the Christians he knew back in Persia had told him that another Prophet would appear soon but died before they could travel to Arabia.

2. It is interesting that you read so many views on this issue. From all my education and research, I have not seen any discussion that it didn't happen, or that it was one mass hallucination, or that he was crucified but survived. The only Islamic opinion I have seen is that Jesus himself was not actually crucified, but rather it only appeared that he was. Now there IS some speculation among Muslim scholars if the person on the cross was an illusion, or a simulacrum created by God, or one of Jesus's disciples ... but that is as far as it goes.

3. Music has traditionally been one of the more controversial issues in the Muslim world. While all Muslim scholars have always accepted and even encouraged chanting the

call to prayer and the Qur'an, the permissibility of other forms of music, especially instrumental music, has been disputed. There are three circles of understanding, one inside the other:

a. The largest circle, that which ALL Muslims agree upon, is that the content and context of any music performance must be in line with Islamic morality. The content means lyrics. Singing is the same as speech and poetry. So songs and poems should be have true, righteous words and be free of anything vulgar, lewd, abusive, or promoting of sin. The context means the way the song is performed and the setting it is performed in. The theme of the song may be good, but the performance of the singer — through soft speech or suggestive movements — may make it prohibited. Also, singing should not be accompanied with something that is prohibited such as alcohol, nakedness, or mixing of men with women as is common in pubs and nightclubs.

b. The medium circle, that which most (but not all) moderate Muslims promote, is that in addition to the conditions of #1, the content of the music should not include any wind or string musical instruments. Some allow all percussion instruments, and some allow only the hand-drum.

c. The smallest circle, that which most (but not all) conservative Muslims promote, is that in addition to the conditions of #2, the hand-drum can only be played by women and only for specific celebrations, such as Eid, weddings, celebrating a new baby, and welcoming a returning traveler.

These are the views found in Islamic thought.

4. Jihad is spiritual in general and physical in particular. Jihad means "struggle," so the general meaning is "struggling" against the evil temptations the self and of Satan. However, in particular cases related to social justice and establishing security, it also means speaking out against oppression and injustice. This known as "Jihad of the Tongue" or "Jihad of the Pen." However, Islam does permit its followers to bear arms to and mobilize armies for the community's defense, to stop aggression and persecution, and to establish security in the land so people can live without fear.

The verses that mention "ambush" and "preparing to attack" the disbelievers was revealed in the context of the Meccan pagans who had signed a peace treaty with the Muslims of Medina and then broke it by ambushing one of the non-Muslim tribes that had allied with Medina. This act of treachery is why God commanded the Muslims of that time to go on the offensive and fight these pagans until they were subdued. These verses are not a general commandment, because elsewhere in the Qur'an it says: **If the enemy sues for peace, then incline to peace.** Therefore, Muslim scholars understand that in general, a Muslim political body should honor all overtures to ceasefires and peace agreements, and that only in specific cases of previous treachery does the Muslim authority have the option of "ambush" and "preparing to attack."

5. There are many views on abortion in Islam, just as in Christianity. However, the majority justify abortion in the first trimester if and only if dire necessity can be proven by the woman's doctor. This is based on a known Saying of the Prophet in which he said that God sends an angel to breathe the soul into the fetus 120 days after conception. So these scholars use this to mean that abortions before that time do not actually entail killing a human being. However, "abortion on demand" is not widely supported even among liberal scholars; hence the requirement for a doctor to bear witness that the woman will suffer physical or emotional harm if she carries the baby to term.

6. This verse is a hot topic. You are correct that the general teachings of honoring women and mothers belie this surface translation. The best answer I can give you is a nice short talk by one of my favorite Islamic speakers, Nouman Ali Khan:
http://podcast.bayyinah.com/2016/10/11/hitting-women-thats-messed-up-nouman-ali-khan/

7. You are correct on this. Slavery was widespread when Islam was revealed, so there are rules regulating it and spelling out what is acceptable behavior for those who had slaves. Since Islam is a practical religion, abolishing slavery in one commandment would have caused more problems than it solved.

So instead of changing the status of these captives and slaves, it changed the treatment and rights of captives and slaves.

Islam forbids one to harm those under his authority. The Prophet (peace be upon him) forbade causing physical harm to slaves: *Hilal b. Yasaf reported that a person got angry and slapped his slave-girl. Thereupon Suwaid b. Muqarrin said to him: See I was one of the seven sons of Muqarrin, and we had only one slave-girl. The youngest of us slapped her, and Allah's Messenger (may peace be upon him) commanded us to set her free.* [Sahih Muslim, Book 015, Number 4082]

In another narration, the Prophet (peace be upon him) said, *"Your slaves are your brothers and Allah has put them under your command. So whoever has a brother under his command should feed him of what he eats and dress him of what he wears. Do not ask them (slaves) to do things beyond their capacity and if you do so, then help them."*

If the Prophet (peace be upon him) forbade slapping slaves, then it's unthinkable that he would have permitted raping them. It just makes no sense. Since rape is a form of harm, it follows that rape is forbidden. Permitting a man to sleep with his slave-girl is in the same category of permitting a man to have multiple wives: an option for dealing humanely and justly with the social and community realities that existed at the time of revelation.

8. Sheikh Hani al-Jubayr, former judge of the Jeddah Supreme Court of Saudi Arabia has said the following:

If the non-Muslim country did not attack the Muslim one nor mobilize itself to prevent the practice and spread of Islam, nor transgress against mosques, nor work to oppress the Muslim people in their right to profess their faith and decry unbelief, then it is not for the Muslim country to attack that country. Jihad of a military nature was only permitted to help Muslims defend their religion and remove oppression from the people.

The Persians and Romans did in fact aggress against Islam and attack the Muslims first. The Chosroe of Persia had gone so far as to order his commander in Yemen specifically to kill the Prophet (peace be upon him). The Romans mobilized their forces to fight the Prophet (peace be upon him), and the Muslims confronted them in the Battles of Mu'tah and Tabûk during the Prophet's lifetime.

The early Muslims lived in a time when the default status of countries was to be "at war" until there was a formal "peace treaty." We now live in a world where the default status is to be "at peace" until there is a "declaration of war." It is not Islam that spread by violence; rather it is the Muslim empire that spread this way. What I mean is that we must not confuse the political expansion of the Arabs through warfare with the religious expansion of Islam. The political powers of the time lived by maxim "conquer or be conquered," and the Muslim powers lived the same way. They were playing the same "Great Game" as the rest of the civilizations around them.

9. Correct, there are no verses or Hadiths condoning the death penalty for apostasy. The Prophet said that only those who *"changed their faith and betrayed the community"* were liable to the death penalty. That second part "betrayed" means only treason was a capital crime. There were many people during the Prophet's life that accepted Islam and then renounced it, and he did not order anything about that person. It was only when one man defected to the Meccan side during the war between Mecca and Medina that the Prophet made this command. So the point is that this apostasy ruling is specifically for treason against the Muslim country, not changes in a person's conscience.

Apologies for the long-winded email, but the topics are important enough to warrant a comprehensive approach. Looking forward to your response and to continuing the dialogue!

May peace be with you,
Ahmed

Why Islam?

Islamic Theology and History: Part 2

Email #04 – From: Rene
Sent: Monday, March 13, 2017 9:14 p.m.

Hello Mr. Rashed,

Thank you for your answers to my questions. I really do appreciate the time that you have taken for this, your references, and detailed responses. I do have additional questions. I apologize if some of these seem silly, frivolous, or unimportant.

If there is no halal food available, would it still be considered unlawful if someone were to eat food considered haram in order to survive? Is it preferable to eat vegetarian or vegan food to eating non-halal meats? I imagine this is the case; in any regard, a vegetarian or vegan diet is arguably healthier.

Is it considered haram to enter the worship spaces of other religions? Would it be forbidden to engage in holidays belonging to these religions if they are observed in a secular manner? For example, my family does not observe the Christian Easter in the traditional religious sense due to its pagan origins; rather, it is celebrated as a time to be together as a family, enjoy a special meal, and the coming of spring after a long winter. Is this okay?

Regarding the marriage between Muhammad and Aisha— my conscience condemned this until I delved a bit deeper into the historical context, realizing that unions between older men and young girls were common in ancient times in most communities, and was hardly unique to Islam. In fact, it continued even within Christianity into the Middle Ages, if memory serves. However, I have been told that marriages between grown men and very young girls are still allowed and practiced. Is this the case?

What are the major differences between the various denominations of Islam, Sunni, Shia, Qur'anist, and Sufi Islam?

Are Hadith considered equal in authority to the Qur'an? Do views on this vary by denomination?

What kind of authority do imams have? Do views on this vary by denomination?

What is this about seventy-two virgins being given to each man who reaches Paradise? Is there a reason that this has sometimes been translated as *seventy-two raisins*? I understand that there is some controversy about this, so I look forward to receiving your answer.

I am curious as to whether or not there is any scientific or historical evidence of mankind having been sixty cubits, or ninety feet tall, as it is said Adam was?

Is the story of Adam and Eve more or less the same as the version told in the Torah/Bible, other than that Eve is not blamed for the introduction of sin into the world?

If Adam and Eve were created and gave birth to sons and daughters (per Gen. 5:4; elsewhere only three sons are named — Cain, Seth, and the murdered Abel), and no other humans were created by God except through normal human reproduction, does this not mean that the children of Adam and Eve committed incest in order to produce more humans, and that God apparently condoned this, despite the fact that such an act is forbidden and abhorred in both the Torah and the Qur'an?

Is Zoroaster considered a prophet in Islam (or does he have no place within the religion whatsoever)?

About the spiritual entities called jinn — what exactly are they? I have read that they are spirits, some demons, some benevolent, some malevolent, that they are capable of some interference within human affairs, as well as possession, etc.

In response to your answer for my seventh question in the previous email: I understand what you are saying. To forbid slapping or striking a slave, only to condone and even allow rape, does not make sense. My only issue is how could it not be considered rape or coercion, considering the fact that these women are slaves, taken as spoils of war? Why on earth would they want to sleep with these men, especially given the fact that it is likely that a great deal of them were already married and probably still had living husbands?

Are household, health, and beauty items such as soap or cosmetics that are vegan (do not contain animal products) but do contain alcohol, haram? I have read conflicting opinions on this, and therefore I'm not sure what to believe on this.

Is it ever acceptable to say the five daily prayers in one's native tongue? In this same vein, under what conditions is it acceptable to miss a prayer, but to either pray it before its due time or to make it up at a later time?

This is undoubtedly the most difficult question for any religious person, any God-believing person, to answer. I know this from firsthand experience. I was raised as a Christian, and many times atheist or agnostic friends posed this question to me. For a long time, I could not answer; later, I relied on the strictly Christian concept of "original/ancestral sin" — that is, claiming that through their disobedience, Adam and Eve introduced sin, and therefore the consequences of sin, pain, death, and suffering, into the world — to answer this question. That question is, if God is wholly good, loving, kind, merciful, etc., then why is there so much pain and suffering in this world?

I can understand to some extent why some kinds of suffering exist (i.e., unjust regimes, wars, abuse, etc.), because these kinds are created and caused by humans. But what about those who are suffering in poverty or famine (and not because they are unwilling to work to provide for themselves and/or their family, but because, even with all of that work, they still do not have enough)? What about those who are born with a physical or mental disability or contract a disease? I have read many times from several different religions that "God works in mysterious ways," or certain kinds of suffering are some sort of "test of faith." In some instances, I can understand this through personal experiences in which I did suffer and was thence brought closer to God; but this is not always the case, and in many instances suffering is meaningless and empty. Why does God sit back and allow this? I understand that we humans have free will and oftentimes we bring some of our sufferings on ourselves, or these are inflicted by others.

But as for the aforementioned kinds of suffering, like disabilities and disease, we do not bring these on ourselves. And if God has created everything and is responsible for everything, why are so many afflicted with such horrible things?

I can understand someone believing in one God over the Trinity. As someone who was raised as a devout Christian and approached religion from a scholastic point of view, I studied the scriptures, patristics, church history, etc. At an early age I began to see many logical inconsistencies, as well as contradictions, within Christian belief, tradition, and the texts of the New Testament. But why should one believe the religion of Islam over, say, Judaism? I am aware that the earliest Hebrew scriptures are now lost and that the oldest version of the Pentateuch is in the Septuagint, a translation of an earlier Hebrew, which calls into question the text's accuracy and reliability. Is there any evidence that the Qur'an is any more reliable or unaltered and unchanged? And how can anyone be sure that the Hadiths are reliable and accurate testimonies as well? I feel this is very relevant, given the great doctrinal importance placed upon them.

Are there any theories as to why the rewards of the afterlife differ between men and women?

I must apologize for the quantity of these questions. If any of them are worded or phrased insensitively, please forgive me — I do not mean to be in any way offensive or disrespectful toward anyone's belief in the least, especially given that I am entertaining the possibility that these beliefs may be entirely correct. As you have acknowledged in your email, this is irrefutably an extremely difficult process; insofar it has proved confusing, exhausting, and at times emotionally draining. I really do appreciate any answers that you have for me, as well as those which you have already provided.

Sincerely,
Rene

Email #05 – From: Ahmed Rashed
Sent: Monday, March 20, 2017 9:54 a.m.

In the Name of God, Most Gracious, Most Merciful

Good morning Rene,

Please forgive me for taking so long to reply. The snowstorm last week took out our power, and then I got so busy with family and home that I could not get to my computer. No questions are silly, frivolous, or unimportant. Remember, our purpose is to make Islam understandable to YOU. Whatever questions or topics you want to discuss, we are open to them and we hope we can provide the answers you seek.

1. If there is no halal food option, observant Muslims will eat vegetarian or seafood. This is because the Qur'an and the Prophet said that "all that comes from the seas (and rivers) are permissible." So all seafood is permissible without any ritual slaughtering, including shellfish. Mammals and birds are the only animals that are required to be "halal" in the sense of ritual slaughtering. I think this is what you meant by "no halal food available." If you meant the extreme case of being shipwrecked or stuck in the middle of the desert, then all dietary restrictions are suspended until the person gets out of that dire circumstance.

2. It is okay for a Muslim to enter the place of worship of other faiths, as long as they do not participate in them. Observation is fine. Also, since family is so important in Islam and the Prophet's teachings, it is mandatory to maintain ties and kinship with them, even if they are not Muslim. So having a holiday dinner with them is good and encouraged. As you said, if they are "celebrating" in a nonreligious way, being with them is not only permissible, it is required. Only if the non-Muslim family goes to church or temple does the Muslim abstain from the ritual itself. Many converts either skip going altogether in this case or wait in the lobby or wings of the building until the religious ceremony is over. When the people disperse to the coffee and bagels, they go back in and mingle in the social space.

3. First of all, I am very glad the historical context of the Prophet's marriage to Aisha was clear to you. This is usually the toughest part to convey to my readers and listeners. As for today, yes there are some Muslim-majority countries that still have this, but these are actually AGAINST the laws that are on the books. Most have set the minimum marriage age to fourteen or sixteen or eighteen. Even Afghanistan has fourteen as the minimum age for girls to marry (like Madagascar and Paraguay, which have little or no Muslim presence). These are the laws in the countries. Saudi Arabia and many conservative Muslim countries have sixteen as the minimum age and many not-so-conservative Muslim countries have eighteen as the minimum. However, in tribal areas or those places which are still far from developed, very young girls are still married to much older men. This is just because the reach of the central government has not gotten to those remote areas, so they are still living that historical context.

4. The Sunni–Shia split began as a political difference regarding who has the right to lead the Muslim community after the Prophet's death. Shia believed it should be a relative of the Prophet, so they thought Ali (the Prophet's cousin) should assume power. Sunni believed there is no "divine right" to rule, so they thought Abu Bakr (the Prophet's friend and adviser who was considered most suitable for the job) should assume power. Ali and Abu Bakr actually settled their differences before Abu Bakr died. However, this political difference took a religious turn when Ali's son Hussein challenged one of the Muslim rulers and was killed. The religious difference that exists today is very minimal. Both consider the same Qur'an to be from God. As for Sufi, this is a spiritual "new-age" movement that started in the eleventh century as a response to the overly legalistic way of practicing Islam that had become prevalent in that centrury. Sufi orders try to get back to the spirituality of the original followers of the Prophet. They also are not considered much different from the mainstream, since they hold the same beliefs and laws but focus more on spiritual aspects before the legal or ritual aspects.

As for Qur'anis, these are the most "deviated" of the list you gave. They believe that all Sayings of the Prophet are suspect and reject them all, only following the Qur'an. Sunni, Shia, and Sufi don't agree with this because the Qur'an clearly says "obey God and obey the Prophet." There is a complete science of historical narration critique that Sunnis, Shia, and Sufi use to judge whether any Saying or Tradition of the Prophet is authentic, sound, weak, fabricated, or unsubstantiated.

5. The Hadith are considered just as canonical as the Qur'an as long as they do not contradict the Qur'an and do not contradict common sense or the general principles of justice. This is the Sunni, Shia, and Sufi view. Obviously, Qur'anis claim that all Hadith are fabricated, and that is why they reject them all.

6. Sunni and Sufi and Qur'anis consider imams to be nothing more than prayer leaders or scholars. They are fallible human beings who sin and repent, and the only thing that sets them apart is their knowledge of the Qur'an an Islam. This is similar to Jewish rabbis. Shias have a different understanding. In the beginning, "imam" meant someone who was related to or descended from the Prophet and was INFALLIBLE. So they believed that they were just like Prophets in that they do not sin and they still have access to divine revelation. When the twelfth imam died without leaving a son, they developed the idea of occultation, which basically means that twelfth imam is in suspended animation until the Last Days, when he will emerge to battle the Antichrist. After that event, all remaining imams are seen like their Sunni counterparts.

7. *The "72 virgins" idea is probably the most overblown idea that people seem to remember about Islam. It's turning into a real stereotype. Forget the doctrines of monotheism and tolerance — it seems all people want to hear about is the virgins. There's a lot more to Paradise than just sex and physical pleasure, you know.* The above is actually a quote from Sheila Musaji, chief editor of *The American Muslim*. Her article covers this topic very comprehensively:

http://theamericanmuslim.org/tam.php/features/articles/72_virgins_in_paradise/0013172

8. I have not found any credible historical or scientific evidence that mankind was ever sixty cubits tall.

9. The story of Adam and Eve in the Qur'an has two major differences compared to the Biblical narration. First, there is debate in Muslim scholarly circles whether this garden was in "heaven" or just some high place here on earth. The majority conclude that it was an earthly paradise because of the existence of sin and temptation. The second difference is that both Adam and Eve sinned and both repented, and both were forgiven. The Qur'an teaches that their descent to the regular Earth was part of God's plan. He intended to make them and their offspring stewards of the Earth, and this descent was the next step in their spiritual development.

10. Muslim scholars quote the Midrashic tradition for this. Adam and Eve had twins (boy and girl) each time they conceived. God instructed the boy of one set to marry the girl of the other set, and this is how the first few generations of people came about. So Abel had a twin sister and Cain had a twin sister. They were supposed to marry the "other" twin's sister, but Cain preferred his own twin. This is the reason Adam suggested they make an offering to God to let Him judge the request. God accepted Abel's offering but not Cain's, and that was one of the reasons why Cain became jealous of his brother and killed him. Jews and Muslims both state that this kind of incest was allowed only in the beginning and then disallowed as time went by.

11. It is possible Zoroaster was a divinely inspired prophet, but it is also possible that he was not. The Qur'an says that **"some messengers we told you about, and others we did not tell you about,"** so most Muslim scholars consider him a prophet because of the core of monotheism in Zoroastrianism.

12. Islam teaches that all paranormal phenomena —ghosts, goblins, haunting, possession, poltergeists, seances, spirit-channeling, and most psychic powers — are explained by the jinn. Jinn are creatures created after angels but before humans.

Like the angels, they are part of the Unseen World; however, like humans, they have free will and they eat, drink,

procreate, grow old, and die. On the Day of Judgment, they will be called to account for their faith and deeds like humans. There are good, believing jinn and there are evil, wicked jinn. You can find a detailed explanation of the jinn and how they interact with humans in these links:
http://www.islamreligion.com/articles/669/world-of-jinn-part-1
http://www.islamreligion.com/articles/674/world-of-jinn-part-2/

You can also check out these books on the topic:

Ibn Taymeyah's Essay On The Jinn (Demons): 2nd Edition (Abu Ameenah Bilal Philips)

The Exorcist Tradition in Islam (Abu Ameenah Bilal Philips)

13. Critics say that it's unthinkable that female slaves back then would have willingly consented to having sex with their Muslim captors who just killed their family members. However, these critics are ignorant of history, for female slaves did consent to having sex with their captors back in the past.

John McClintock said: *"Women who followed their father and husbands to the war put on their finest dresses and ornaments previous to an engagement, in the hope of finding favor in the eyes of their captors in case of a defeat."* (John McClintock, James Strong, "Cyclopedia of Biblical, Theological, and Ecclesiastical Literature" [Harper & Brothers, 1894, p. 782).

Matthew B. Schwartz said: *"The Book of Deuteronomy prescribes its own rules for the treatment of women captured in war [Deut 21:10-14] . Women have always followed armies to do the soldiers' laundry, to nurse the sick and wounded, and to serve as prostitutes. They would often dress in such a way as to attract the soldiers who won the battle. The Bible recognizes the realities of the battle situation in its rules on how to treat female captives, though commentators disagree on some of the details. The biblical Israelite went to battle as a messenger of God. Yet he could also, of course, be caught up in the raging tide of blood and violence. The Western mind associates prowess, whether military or athletic, with sexual success. The pretty girls crowd around the hero who scores the winning touchdown, not around the players of the losing team. And it is certainly true in war: the winning hero 'attracts' the women."* (Matthew B. Schwartz, Kalman J. Kaplan, *The Fruit of Her Hands:*

The Psychology of Biblical Women [Wm. B. Eerdmans Publishing, 2007, pp. 146-147).

Thus we see from two non-Muslim authors that female slaves back in the past would consent to having sex with their captors, and the Qur'an was sent to address the issues of **that societal context**. So if we put aside our twenty-first century mindset and look at history objectively, there is nothing wrong with saying that female slaves back then consented to having sex with their captors, and it is perfectly reasonable to conclude that the Muslims did not rape their female slaves, *especially since they were forbidden from harming those under their care or authority*.

Even if **some** of the Muslims back then did rape their female slaves, this would only show that they committed a **sinful** act ... NOT that the Prophet (peace be upon him) approved of such behavior. So the discussion is about consensual sex between master and slave not about rape.

If Islam allows a man to have multiple wives as long as each wife consents and he provides equal time and money to each, why should he not be allowed to cohabit with slave women in his possession, since he is providing the same care to them and they are living in the same quarters *and they agree to such intimacy*?

Notice that Islam is practical. Most people would agree that having unrelated men and women in the same living quarters for extended time would often lead to sexual attraction. That is human nature. So Islam gives women, whether free or slave, the right to their bodies while also allowing them appropriate outlets for their sexuality. If she doesn't want her master to approach her, she can stay aloof from him. In fact, Turkish and Mughal literature is filled with references to masters writing poetry and songs to try to woo their female slaves. That shows that the master-slave dynamic in Islamic culture was not as tyrannical as many expect. This is the result of the requirement to treat them humanely and with compassion and fairness.

14. Most scholars say that products that contain alcohol but are not used for consumption are permissible. A minority say they are prohibited. Also, some scholars also allow alcohol even in

consumables as long as it is medicinal (like cough syrup). One of the blessings of Islam is that as long as there is an authentic scholarly opinion backed up by textual proof, a Muslim can adopt whichever ruling they wish.

15. When a Muslim stands for their ritual prayer, the Qur'an must be recited in original Arabic. Only new converts may recite in their native tongue and only for as long as it takes them to learn the opening chapter of the Qur'an in Arabic (seven verses) and one other short chapter (three verses). After this "grace period" it is expected that all new converts will recite at least these ten verses in original Arabic. Also, the short one-line supplications said when bowing, standing, and prostrating must be said in Arabic. However, all additional supplications that are said when bowing and prostrating can be said in any language. As for missing prayer, any prayer that is missed should be said as soon as the Muslim realizes they missed it. So if you don't wake up for the dawn prayer, you pray as soon as you wake up and realize this. If you couldn't pray the midday prayer because of work or study or whatnot, you pray as soon as you come home.

16. You basically asked, "What does Islam say about the Problem of Evil?" This can be a long discussion, so instead of overloading you with full philosophical breakdown, I'll just give you a highlight and you can ask further questions to develop the details you care about.

The Qur'an mentions in several places that God (Allah) created death and life to test us **"which of you are best in deeds."** So the actual PURPOSE of life is not eat or drink or be merry, but rather to experience the spectrum of happiness and sorrow (and therefore pain and suffering) to put the human soul to trial and so form a basis for judgement in the hereafter. Also, in many places the Qur'an says that **"God does not burden a soul with more than it can bear,"** so Muslims understand that no pain or suffering will be beyond a person's ability to handle it.

That is brief highlight of how Islam sees evil, suffering, and pain in life. We can delve into more detail in a follow-up email if you wish.

17. Yes, that is the very name of our website, Why Islam? So a person has doubts about their faith (any faith), but why would a person consider Islam? What makes Islam have a stronger "truth-claim" than any other religion? If you ask any thoughtful Muslim why they are Muslim, they will invariably reply the same way: "Because Islam is the only religion that has rational and compelling evidence that it is the truth."

This is a big statement, and for someone from a Christian background, it may even sound preposterous. How can rational evidence be compatible with faith? Well, first of all, Islam teaches that God created us and gave us the gift of intellect; therefore, our reasoning should support our faith, not diminish it. Secondly, we must be aware of blindly applying reason without a plan or methodology.

Let us start with an example. Almost all of us have been faced with the questioning of a child. He can be very frustrating to us as he asks "Why?" over and over again. If you put a knife beyond his reach, he wants to know, "Why?" When you explain it is sharp, he asks "Why?" And so you explain, "In order to cut fruit," and he asks, "Why?" And so it goes.

This illustrates the dilemma of applying reason. What we have to do when we apply reason is first to set standards of proof. We decide for ourselves, "What will I be satisfied with if I find such and such and so and so that constitutes for me a final proof?" We have to decide on that **first**. What usually happens is that on the really important issues, the philosophical matters, we tend to ask for proof before deciding on our standards. We may arrive at the point that would constitute a proof, but then we ask for a proof of the proof.

The key to avoiding endless dissatisfaction is to decide about standards first; to satisfy ourselves that such and such are a list of criteria that constitute proof, satisfying proof, and then we test the subjects that we examine. In particular, I will apply this to the Qur'an. Ask a thoughtful Christian why he is a Christian, and he will usually reply, "The miracle of the Resurrection."

The basis for his belief is that about two thousand years ago a man died and was raised from the dead. That is his miracle — his "touchstone" — because all else depends on that. Ask a Muslim, "Well, what is your miracle? Why are you a Muslim?" and the Muslim can go over and take his miracle off the shelf and hand it over to you because his miracle is still with us today. It is the Qur'an; it is his "touchstone."

There are many indications or proofs that a person might use to validate his or her belief that the Qur'an really is from God. Since this email is already very long, here is a link about the authenticity of the Prophet:

http://www.islamkorea.com/english/proof5.html

Also, I have attached an article about the preservation of the Prophet's Sayings.

(Editor's note: See Appendix A for attached article.)

18. See the article linked to question #7.

I hope this addresses your questions. Please forgive the long length, but I like to be comprehensive in my replies. Also, do not be afraid of offending me. Believe me; I have dealt with MUCH worse. I understand this process is emotionally draining, and I am sensitive to that. We are here to help shed light on our faith, so feel free to reply if you have further questions on these topics or any new topics. I look forward to continuing the conversation. However, given the length of this email and the number of links and articles I've attached, I completely understand if it takes a few weeks to hear from you again. May God guide you on your search for Truth.

May peace be with you,
Ahmed Rashed

The Muslim Lifestyle
Email #06 – From: Rene
Sent: Friday, April 14, 2017 10:26 p.m.

Good evening, Mr. Rashed:

First of all, I must thank you for all of the time and effort you have put into answering each and every one of my questions. You've been incredibly patient and helpful with me, and for that I am very grateful. There is absolutely no need to apologize for the delayed response. I asked nearly twenty questions, after all.

Your answers have been incredibly helpful to me and have dispelled a lot of incorrect notions that I have accumulated over the years.

I still have some questions — not quite as difficult to answer as some of the previous, however.

This question is in reference to the Jummah prayer (not sure if that is correct spelling or terminology; if not, please forgive me the error). If there is no mosque within reasonable distance, is it ever permissible for one to simply pray at home? If so, are there certain guidelines or procedures that must be followed?

What are some of the rules (for lack of a better word) of hygiene in Islam? I understand the obvious — general good hygiene, as well as ablutions before prayers. What of certain aspects of personal grooming and the like, such as hair trimming, plucking/shaping of eyebrows, etc.?

What is this about it being impermissible for a Muslim to pet/touch a dog? I completely understand what I've read about ensuring one has no pet hair or anything on their clothing for prayer (I don't think anyone really wants to walk around with pet hair clinging to them regardless of what they are doing, let alone prayer/worship), however.

Why does the Black Stone hold such significance for Muslims?

Why Islam?

It has always been my understanding that, like the vast majority of religions, Islam does not permit lying — rather, it condemns it. However, I have come across some things that seem to contradict that, and I would like your opinion and any background information you may have regarding these things, as it is entirely possible that I am misunderstanding them or interpreting them incorrectly and/or out of context. They are Hadith I have read online — these are the particular Hadith I am referring to: Sahih Bukhari (49:857); Sahih Bukhari (84:64-65); Sahih Muslim (32:6303); Sahih Bukhari (50:369).

I look forward to reading your responses as well as to the edification I'll receive. Thank you again for continuing dialogue with me and for so thoroughly and patiently answering my questions.

Sincerely,
Rene

Email #07 – From: Ahmed Rashed
Sent: Monday, May 8, 2017 7:20 a.m.

Good morning, Rene.

Please forgive the extended delay in responding. For some reason, your email went to my spam folder, and I only saw it late last week. As for time and effort, that is what we are here for, to set the record straight and help people understand what Islam is really all about.

To proceed with your questions:

1. Juma'ah prayer is only obligatory for male residents. Juma'ah is recommended but optional for male travelers, and all women and children. Having said that, many women prefer to stay connected to the community, so they try to go at least once per month as their schedule and ability permit. However, there is no blame or sin on missing the Juma'ah for them. If a Muslim man or woman cannot attend Juma'ah for whatever reason, they pray the midday prayer as usual: four units of bowing — also known as *raka'ah* in Arabic.

2. The rules of hygiene in Islam are summarized by the following Saying of the Prophet: *"Five things are part of the natural way: shaving the pubic hair, circumcision, trimming the mustache, plucking the armpit hairs, and cutting the nails."*

In practice, the followers of the Prophet shave or pluck their pubic and underarm hair. Also, they trim their nails regularly. Tradition states that no more than forty days should elapse between shaving/trimming, but most Muslims today do so every week or two. Of course, circumcision and trimming the mustache is only required for men. In addition, the Prophet recommended his followers to take a full-body bath at least once per week, preferably on Friday morning.

Finally, since you bring up the topic of eyebrows, the Prophet prohibited any kind of "body-changing" such as tattoos, artificial teeth separation, and eyebrow shaving or plucking. These were common forms of beautification in the seventh century, and the Prophet emphasized that the natural human body should not be altered to fit cultural fashions. It may seem strange that removing underarm hair and pubic hair is allowed but removing eyebrow hair is not. The rationale is that the former is a hygiene issue whereas the latter is a vanity issue.

3. Dogs in Islam are commonly misunderstood. Most Muslim scholars agree that in Islam the saliva of a dog is ritually impure and that contact with a dog's saliva requires one to wash seven times. This ruling comes from the Hadith: *"If a dog licks the vessel of any one of you, let him throw away whatever was in it and wash it seven times."* (Reported by Muslim)

It is to be noted, however, that one of the major Islamic schools of thought, the Maliki School, indicates this is not a matter of ritual cleanliness but simply a common-sense method way to prevent the spread of disease. So most modern Muslims, while aware that only the saliva of a dog may be impure, prefer to keep dogs separated form the living quarters of humans, and wash up after playing or touching a dog if that dog's saliva came into contact with them. As far as I know, there is no problem with petting a dog or ruffling its fur; it is only the saliva that triggers the necessity of cleaning. Here are two good articles on this topic if you want further details.

https://www.thoughtco.com/dogs-in-islam-2004392
http://www.virtualmosque.com/islam-studies/faqs-and-fatwas/mans-best-friend-the-islamic-view-on-dogs/

4. Islamic tradition holds that the Black Stone fell from Paradise to show Adam and Eve where to build an altar, which became the first temple on Earth. Muslims believe that the stone was originally pure and dazzling white, but has since turned black because of the sins of the people who touch it. According to a Prophetic tradition, *"Touching them both* (the Black Stone and the Yamani Corner) *is expiation for sins."* Adam's altar and the stone were said to have been lost during Noah's Flood and forgotten. Ibrahim was said to have later found the Black Stone at the original site of Adam's altar when the angel Gabriel revealed it to him. Ibrahim ordered his son Ismael — who in Muslim belief is an ancestor of Muhammad — to build a new temple, the Kaaba, into which the stone was to be embedded.

A Hadith records that, when the second Caliph, Umar ibn al-Khattab (580–644) came to kiss the stone, he said in front of all assembled, *"No doubt, I know that you are a stone and can neither harm anyone nor benefit anyone. Had I not seen Allah's Messenger [Muhammad] kissing you, I would not have kissed you."*

5. Lying is sinful in general. The Prophet strongly condemned lying about God or the Messengers, lying in buying or selling, lying to children to get them to do something, lying for joke or play, and lying when giving testimony. There are only three circumstances when it is permissible, and even then, the lie must be minor and with the intention of greater good. The first exception is in wartime: there is no sin on a Muslim if he or she lies to misdirect the enemy or to protect one's army and country. This is an easy one to understand and see the wisdom behind. The next two are somewhat more controversial: reconciling between two disputing parties and a husband lying to his wife or vice versa for the sake of love and harmony.

It was narrated from Umm Kalthum Bint 'Uqbah that she heard the Messenger say, *"He who reconciles between people by saying something good is not a liar."* (al-Bukhari, 2546; Muslim, 2605)

It was narrated that Asma' Bint Yazeed said, *"The Messenger of Allah (peace and blessings of Allah be upon him) said: 'It is not permissible to tell lies except in three (cases): when a man speaks to his wife in a way to please her; lying in war; and lying in order to reconcile between people.'"*

So these two other cases basically mean there is no sin on a Muslim if he or she tells a minor lie to reconcile between two friends or family members. This could mean either hiding a mean statement one made at the other or attributing a nice statement that one never actually made but would allow the relationship to be smoothed over. It also means that if a Muslim tells their spouse something nice and flattering that is not 100% true, it is not considered a sin. Given that these two circumstances happen all the time across all cultures to keep the social fabric from ripping apart, it is seen as a mercy that the Prophet singled out these two forms of lying as acceptable as long as no limits are transgressed.

Good questions! Feel free to send me more or let me know if there is any other topic you would like to discuss.

May peace be with you,
Ahmed

Prayer and Friendships
Email #08 – From: Rene
Sent: Tuesday, May 16, 2017 7:27 p.m.

Good evening, Mr. Rashed:

Thanks again for your detailed answers. So far you have been very helpful to me, and I appreciate it a lot.

I am aware that there are some slight differences in the way that men and women pray. It is my understanding that the words of the prayers remain the same, but that the postures, placement of hands, etc., are slightly different. What are these specific differences, especially in prostration?

Is it acceptable for women to pray in public as men can often be seen doing, or is it preferable for her to postpone the prayer in order to pray in a private place?

Are all prayers said aloud, or are some said silently? Which are said aloud, and which are silent? Is the entire prayer, including the recitation, silent, or only the prayers, with the Qur'an portion recited aloud?

Are heeled shoes for women forbidden? I have read conflicting things on this minor issue. (To be clear, I am not referring to five-inch spike heels or something like that, but a small heel that isn't noisy and doesn't make a lot of noise).

Is it acceptable for Muslim women and girls to have male friends? What of having a relationship in which there is no premarital physical contact, merely talking and spending supervised time together in order to get to know one another better prior to the possible marriage?

Lastly, I've heard some say that women and men should not mix. But what should one do when attending co-ed schools or working a job in which one has both male and female coworkers?

Thank you very much in advance. I appreciate all of the time that you have taken to help and teach me.

Sincerely,
Rene

Email #09 – From: Ahmed Rashed
Sent: Wednesday, May 24, 2017 4:14 p.m.

In the Name of God, the Most Gracious, the Most Merciful

Good afternoon, Rene. I am happy to see that our conversation is of benefit. No need to apologize for long questions; this is what we are here for.

To begin with your first question, the difference you mention is only relevant to the Hanafi school of law. The Hanafi school teaches a woman when standing to place her hands on her chest, whereas the man places them over his navel. Other schools either teach both men and women to leave the hands at the sides (Maliki) or both men and women to place their hands on the chest (Hanbali and Shafi). When prostrating, the Hanafi school teaches that a woman lets her stomach touch her thighs and lets her elbows touch her ribs, whereas a man leaves a space between his stomach and thighs and between his elbows and ribs. Other schools teach both men and women to leave space between stomach and thigh and between elbows and ribs. A Muslim may follow any school of thought, so it is the individual's choice whether to pray in the Hanafi style or the majority style.

Women are allowed to pray in public as long as their backs are covered and there is no fear of being accosted or attacked. The postures of the prayer are positions of humility, so a woman might be harmed by malicious passersby who take these postures of humility as a sign of weakness or vulnerability. My wife has often prayed by herself at airports and when she was in college.

As for the prayer itself, the supplications of bowing, sitting, and prostrating are always said silently. The *"Allahu Akbar"* one says between postures is always vocalized, but it is only said very loudly when one is leading a congregational prayer. The recitation of the Qur'an is recited loud and clear for the sunset (*maghreb*), night (*isha*), and dawn (*fajr*) prayers and recited silently for the midday (*dhuhr*) and afternoon (*asr*) prayers. For the voluntary night prayers, the person has a choice of whether to recite out loud or silently.

Heeled shoes are not forbidden in principle. They are only prohibited when the heels are high enough to make a woman's walk draw attention to her hips. But since that is what high heels were designed to do, many but not all Muslim women avoid them. Flats and low heels are usually worn without issues.

Friendships between men and women who are not related to each other are strongly discouraged. The Prophet said, *"When a man and a woman are alone together, the Devil is the third."* There is simply too much temptation for the relationship to develop into something more intimate. However, there are some Muslims who do have friends of the opposite sex, so not everyone abides by this norm. Sometimes you will find those who have common family will socialize with each other, but even those are usually only in a large family setting and not in a one-on-one setting. As for courtship and getting-to-know period before marriage, then yes, that does happen a lot. The man and woman who are exploring the possibility of marriage will usually set up some time to meet and talk in a supervised setting (usually the woman's family or friends) to see if their personalities and life goals are compatible for marriage.

Having said all that, how do Muslims usually deal with the opposite sex in a work or education environment? It is not anything exotic or complicated. Muslims are allowed to interact normally; they just keep things professional and do not cross any personal space or have any personal conversations. While of course there are conservative and liberal views on this matter, most Muslim scholars would agree that any conversation that is part of getting the job done is acceptable. Fraternization and socialization is usually not acceptable. In a learning environment, some scholars would say that sitting in the same classroom is okay, but studying together without anyone present is probably not okay. My view is that if the situation looks sketchy or feels sketchy, then it probably IS sketchy, and the Muslim would be best to avoid that situation.

May peace be with you,
Ahmed

Understanding the Prophetic Traditions
Email #10 – From: Rene
Sent: Thursday, June 22, 2017 4:35 a.m.

Good evening, Mr. Rashed:

I have read over your detailed answers and have also been doing some research and reading on my own. I have a few final concerns that I am certain you are far better equipped to answer than, say, Google.

My concern is that it appears in certain places within the Qur'an and Hadith that God is making special concessions for Prophet Muhammad. Now, this in and of itself is not concerning to me, but I don't understand why the scriptures are peppered with such statements of special privilege, etc., when I have never found any such thing in any religious scriptures I've encountered in the past, including that of the other Abrahamic religions.

Such examples as Qur'an 66:1-2, in which Muhammad is permitted to continue sleeping with his female slave Mary the Copt despite his wives' outrage over this — in fact, God rebukes him for having decided to cease his relations with the aforementioned woman in order to appease their jealousy. In 33:53, God prohibits dinner guests from arriving early or staying late when coming to Muhammad's home for dinner, as he is apparently too shy to make his preferences regarding guests coming clear himself. Again, his doing this is not the problem; rather, I don't understand why it should be included within scripture that is meant to apply to all of mankind, not a select group of dinner guests. The verse doesn't seem to be applicable in any way to the present day or Muslims in general.

Another thing I find a bit strange comes from the Hadith and the Qur'an as well. Firstly, the allowance made for Muhammad only to marry more than the maximum of four wives. I have heard the argument that he did not have a romantic or sexual relationship with all of them. It is said that he took these widowed women under his protection and legitimized his taking care of and sheltering them through marriage, yet Sahih al-Bukhari 268 suggests otherwise.

The second, his desire to marry what was technically his daughter-in-law, Zainab, daughter of his adopted son Zaid, an allowance for which is made in Qur'an 33:37. Even Aisha seems to think that some of these things are strangely convenient, saying, "I feel that your Lord hastens in fulfilling your wishes." The confusion as to why so many concessions are made for Muhammad by God throughout scripture and Hadiths stems from the fact that I don't know of such things being done for any of the other Abrahamic prophets recognized by all three Abrahamic religions. Then again, I do recognize that those scriptures are men's writing. God is not speaking in the first person; rather, he is quoted or spoken about throughout, amidst parables, histories, etc. I would appreciate it if you could shed a little light on this matter.

Lastly is the Hadith Sahih al-Bukhari 3329, in which Muhammad answers the questions of Abdullah bin Salam, stating that he has received the answers from the angel Gabriel. Now, the first two answers cannot be disputed, since they have not yet happened, and thus we cannot know their accuracy or inaccuracy. However, the third answer can and is disputed. It is simply not scientifically accurate. Muhammad states that, according to Gabriel, a child resembles whichever parent discharged first during intercourse. In this modern age, we know that this is incorrect. I wouldn't care so much about this if it weren't for the fact that it is clearly false, which brings me to question the accuracy of more important, pertinent statements. Perhaps there is an explanation, especially for one who can read the original Arabic versus this English translation I am reading from. I look forward to your responses to my final set of questions.

I apologize if it seems like each message is an interrogation of sorts; it's just that the truth is of utmost importance to me, as it should be to all people, and thus I want to ensure that I am in fact following truth. A person's hereafter is the most important thing, and thus I want to be certain that in accepting Islam, I am making the right decision. Thank you very much again; please take care.

Blessings to you and to your family,

Rene

Email #11 – From: Ahmed Rashed
Sent: Monday, July 3, 2017 2:14 p.m.

In the Name of God, the Most Gracious, the Most Merciful

Good afternoon, Rene. Let us address your last question first. Remember I told you a few emails ago that the Hadith are considered just as canonical as the Qur'an **as long as they do not contradict the Qur'an and do not contradict common sense or the general principles of justice**. The Sayings of the Prophet (*Hadiths*) were officially compiled in the authenticated volumes, or the Sahih Volumes, over two hundred years after his death. This means that it is quite possible that many Hadiths that we have today are not in their original forms. They had been altered, either intentionally or unintentionally. Much of the writings of the Hadiths' volumes were also written by the scholars' students and their students.

So even with the best of intentions and efforts, the transmissions are prone to error, and some Hadiths do contain errors. So if there is a scientific error in a given Hadith, it may not necessarily be from the Prophet. This particular Hadith is classified as *ahad*, not *mutawatir*. The former means "singular" and refers to the fact that it was recorded with only one chain of narrators. The latter means "plural" and refers to the fact that it was recorded with **multiple** chains of narrators and therefore has more historical weight that it was actually said by the Prophet. This is one strike against taking this Hadith seriously, even if it is in Bukhari.

Another strike against it is that it is not a Hadith that deals with belief, worship, or law. Why does this matter? Well, there is a little-known fact outside of Islamic scholarly circles that Bukhari and Muslim and their students were very, very careful of vetting Hadiths that dealt with the above topics. They would check the chain of narrators for any flaw or issue, and they would check the meaning of the Hadith itself for consistency against other similar Hadiths and the Qur'an. However, Hadiths that dealt with simply historical events, or people, or even heart-softening advice were not vetted with this level of critical analysis.

That is why the Hadith scholar I talked to about this Hadith replied dismissively. He confirmed my suspicion that there is no harm in rejecting this particular Hadith since 1) it talks about the natural world in a way that is inaccurate, 2) it was transmitted to us with only a "singular" chain of narrators, and 3) it does not fall in the "big three" categories of well-vetted Sayings. He also pointed out something very important: there is **another** narration of the Prophet's answer but with **different** wording. In your narration, the original Arabic text uses the word *sabaqat*, which means "precedes" or "surpasses" or "outstrips." He pointed out that translator chose the word "preceded" or "comes before." However, if we look at another Hadith (Sahih Muslim - 314), we find Aisha reporting that the Prophet (pbuh) said, *"... if her water **dominates** the man's water, the child resembles the maternal uncles, but if the water of the man **dominates** her water, the child resembles the paternal uncles."* So the scholar I talked to pointed out that here the original Arabic text uses the word *alaa*, which means "dominates" or "overcame" or "elevated above" or "exalted over."

This second narration is more in line with our current understanding of genetics. First of all, we know from other Hadiths that the Prophet (pbuh) mentioned that the "water" of women is involved in process of fertilization; so it is not an interpretive stretch to say that a woman's "water" is that which contains her genetic information. Likewise, we know from other Hadiths that the Prophet (pbuh) equated the "water" of men with *mani*, which is the Arabic word for semen; so it is easy to interpret a man's "water" as that which contains his genetic information.

Therefore, we can interpret this Hadith to mean that if the genetic information of the one *dominates* or *overcomes* or *supersedes* that of the other, resemblance will follow. From this, my scholar told me, we can see that the first narration would no longer be problematic; we just use the "surpasses" nuance instead of the "precedes" nuance in the original Arabic text.

This is also the first thing my Hadith teacher told me to look for, and the primary reason he admonished me and other Muslims from trying to read Hadiths "on their own" without a teacher to guide them through all the contradictory narrations and how the scholars reconcile them or reject one or accept another. Also, even if we accept a Hadith, we cannot understand it without cross-referencing with other Hadiths. Remember that the collectors of Hadith did their best to sift through the historical Sayings and anecdotes that were attributed to the Prophet and extract the authentic from the baseless. However, these collections (and their translations) are still best-effort work from fallible human beings.

On a personal note, even if this interpretation does not satisfy me, why should I let my faith hang on one or two narrations that are contradictory to each other? If the answers were things only a prophet would know, how would Abdullah bin Salam know the answers were correct, unless he, himself, was also a prophet? If it was a well-known test of prophets, and the answers that should be given were known by people who were not prophets, then it is not much of a test, is it? That is the fourth reason why I would suspend belief in this narration, but not on the Hadith tradition in general, because there are other Hadiths that deal with belief, worship, and law and are "plural" narrations and therefore deserving of my intellectual acceptance, not just my spiritual acceptance.

Unfortunately, it is a common tactic of the old Orientalists and the current Islamophobes to cherry-pick Hadiths with questionable translations from the huge "authentic" corpus and throw them in a Muslim's face to shake their faith. As my teacher instructed me, just because a Hadith is classified as "authentic" does not mean it is accurate; it only means that the chain of narrators did not have any apparent defect, and the meaning of the narration did not have any apparent flaw **at the time of recording.** Only by cross-referencing with other Hadiths and double-checking the information in the Hadith itself and its many interpretive meanings can a Hadith scholar conclude definitively that any given Hadith is historically valid. By the way, this work of reviewing Hadiths is still going on today! Many doctoral students of esteemed Islamic seminaries in Egypt, Turkey, Saudi Arabia, Pakistan, India, and so on often have the review and reclassification of some segment of these old Hadiths as part of their thesis for graduation.

The only text to which I give my complete trust is the Noble Qur'an, because I believe it really is from God Almighty, and I have yet to find anything in history or science or morality or ethics that shakes this touchstone of my faith. Science today has confirmed over and over and over that the Quran's scientific statements are indeed in perfect harmony with science. The historical narrations of the Qur'an have also been mostly verified, from the defeat of the Persians at the hands of the Byzantines in the Prophet's lifetime to the accurate prediction of the Pharaoh of Moses being preserved to correctly identifying the city of Iram that used to trade with 'Ad. Also, it is the only book for which each and every verse is *mutawatir*, so each and every verse has been corroborated by multiple chains of narrators.

Now, let us move on to your next concern: the special concessions the Prophet Muhammad seemed to have received during his life as a Prophet. First, I would like to put to rest the misconception that the Prophet married Zainab out of his own desire that was only later "justified" by revelation.

Abdul Hameed Siddique states in his book: *"So far as the fanciful stories and calumnies of the Orientalists are concerned, we can only say that these are so absurd that anyone having even a grain of sense in him would unhesitatingly reject them as mere fabrications. William Muir and so many others like him state that the Prophet, having seen Zainab by chance through a half-open door, was fascinated by her* beauty, and that Zaid having come to know of the leanings of his master, divorced her and then she was marred to Muhammad. There is absolutely no truth in these stories which have been fabricated in this connection." (*The Life of Muhammad* by Abdul Hameed Siddique, Islamic Publications LTD, p. 214)

The answer given by Abdul Hameed Siddique doesn't really tell us much, so now I will quote from *Sirat-Un-Nabi* by Allama Shibli Nu'Mani: "*Tabari writes that once the Prophet (peace and blessings of God be upon him) visited the house of Zaid. Zaid was not at home, and Zainab was dressing herself. The Prophet (peace and blessings of God be upon him) saw her doing that, and turned back saying, 'Glory to God, Most High and glory to him who turns the hearts.' Zaid came to know of it. He came to the Prophet (peace and blessings of God be upon him) and said, 'I may divorce Zainab if you have come to like her.'*

I have quoted that dirty narration with a pricking of conscience. But to report a blasphemy is not the same as to commit a blasphemy. This is a single report that forms the mainstay of authority for the Christian historians. But the poor fellows do not know what value this narration holds when critically viewed in the light of the principles set by the traditionalists. Tabari has taken this story from **Waqidi***, the well-known* **liar** *and* **fabricator***. He coined such fictions to provide some sort of sanction for the licentiousness of the 'Abbasid caliphs.*" (*Sirat-Un-Nabi*, by Allama Shibli Nu'Mani, rendered into English by M. Tayyib Bahksh Budayuni, Kazi Publications, Lahore, Vol. II, p. 128–129)

In addition, Sheikh Shabir Ally was once asked, "*Is it true that the Prophet (pbuh) had fallen in love with Zainab due to her beauty?*"

He replied, "*If that were true, it would not detract from the veracity of the Prophet. Muslims admit that he was a human being. It is not unnatural for a man to fall in love. The fact that he is a Prophet does not rob him of his natural human emotions. In fact, it is true that he loved all his wives. However, it is not true that he fell in love with Zainab in the way that is claimed by some critics. They say that once the Prophet visited Zaid, the husband of Zainab. Zaid was out at the time, and Zainab was combing her hair. The Prophet was struck by her beauty and immediately left saying something to the effect that God changes the hearts of people. When Zaid learnt about this incident he offered the Prophet that he would divorce Zainab in order that the Prophet may marry her. Accordingly, he divorced her and the Prophet married her.*

Several things point to the lack of truth in this story. First, it is unlikely that the Prophet (pbuh) was suddenly struck by Zainab's beauty. Zainab was his cousin. He had known her since childhood. Why would she suddenly appear striking after she was already married to another?

Second, the Prophet himself had arranged for her to get married to Zaid. If there was to be an attraction, why did the Prophet (pbuh) not encourage her to marry none but himself?

Third, the fact of the matter was that Zaid's marriage proved to be an unhappy one. Zaid was a former slave and as such was held in low esteem in the eyes of Zainab. He mentioned to the Prophet that he intended to divorce his wife, but the Prophet advised him to keep his wife and avoid divorce.

While Zaid intended to divorce his wife, God intended to marry her to the Prophet. Eventually Zaid could maintain his marriage no longer. He divorced Zainab and God declared in his Book that he has wedded her to the Prophet after the proper waiting period was over.

This marriage served more than one purpose. First, the Prophet was responsible for arranging Zainab's marriage to Zaid. In a sense, then, he was also indirectly responsible for the unhappiness she felt in her marriage. Her marriage to the Prophet now provided her the honor she felt she deserved, and exonerated the Prophet.

Second, Zaid had been adopted as the Prophet's son. Eventually, however, the Qur'an prohibited the practice of changing the parental identity of adopted persons. Zaid, then, was to no longer be called 'son of Muhammad' but rather a 'close friend.' The Prophet's marriage to the divorced wife of Zaid was a practical demonstration that the adopted relationship was not equal to a real blood-relationship. A man cannot marry the divorced wife of his real son, but he can marry the divorced wife of his adopted son."

So we see that Zaid was already planning on divorcing Zainab due to the unhappy state of their marriage. We see that the Prophet advised him to keep his wife; this advice is recorded in the Qur'an, by the way. Even Aisha later admonished those who accused her late husband of fabricating or changing the Qur'an to suit his desires. She said, *"If there were a passage of the Qur'an the Prophet would have desired to hide or change, it would have been this one,"* referring to the verses about Zainab and Zaid. Yet the Prophet did not do so, which shows that the Qur'an was out of his control and not for him to change or edit as he wishes.

Now let us discuss how God relates to His Prophets. I argue that Muhammad (pbuh) is not unique in getting special instructions. Prophet Job also received special concessions. When he lost his wealth, health, and children, and his wife pleaded with him to ask God for relief, he got angry and swore an oath to God that if he ever got better, he would beat her one hundred lashes or divorce her. Eventually God cured Job (pbuh) of his ailments, so Job (pbuh) was worried about his oath. A Prophet cannot forswear himself, so he was worried that he would have to divorce his wife, the only person who stood by him during his trials. Obviously, Job did not want to take the other option! God then revealed instructions to Job (pbuh) to take one hundred blades of grass in a bunch and fulfill his oath by tapping his wife with that. So here you have a special concession from God.

Prophet Ibrahim (pbuh) also received special concessions. When he broke all the idols in his father's temple, he left the largest one standing. When the people asked him if he did this, he replied that it was the largest idol that got jealous and destroyed the other idols. The intention was to draw the people's never attention to the absurdity of idolatry. It was still a lie, but he was not punished or reprimanded by God for that. Also, God permitted him to lie about his wife, Sarah, so she would not fall into the hands of that tyrant king. Also, when the angels visited him to inform him they were going to destroy the city of Lot (pbuh), Ibrahim (pbuh) argued with them. God admonished him but did not reprimand him.

Prophet Jacob (pbuh) was allowed to marry both daughters of his maternal uncle. Usually sisters are not allowed to be co-wives, but this concession allowed him to marry both the woman he was attracted to (the younger sister, Rachel) and the woman that his uncle wanted to marry off (the elder sister, Leah). So again you have a special concession from God.

Prophet Moses (pbuh) received many special concessions. After killing a man in Egypt, God guided him to the land of Midian, where he found shelter, work, and a wife and family. During his meeting with God, he asked God to appoint his brother Aaron as a prophet with him, since Aaron was more eloquent in speech. God granted this prayer. Also, when Moses (pbuh) lost his temper on several occasions with the Israelites and his own brother, God forgave him and instructed him how his followers could repent and how he should behave. When Moses (pbuh) made his claim that nobody had more knowledge than him, God instructed him to follow Khidr (the Servant in Sura 18) and learn from him. Even when Moses (pbuh) failed all those tests, still God overlooked that and allowed him to return to his people in a good — albeit more humble — status.

Likewise with the Prophet Muhammad (pbuh), the Qur'an is filled with corrections to the Prophet. Surah 80 was revealed because the Prophet frowned at a blind believer while he was trying to talk to an arrogant tribal chieftain. Surah 66, as you mentioned, was revealed because the Prophet vowed never to approach Maryia the Copt. For the moment, overlook that she was a slave. She had almost the same status as a full-wife, so two of the Prophet's other wives were essentially demanding that he divorce one of his other wives. Even though this is an unjust demand, the Prophet agreed to it to appease these two wives; so God revealed Surah 66 to guide the Prophet as to what was the better choice.

Also, realize that not all special instructions were concessions. In Surah 33, God revealed that the Prophet could not divorce any of his wives or marry new ones. If the Qur'an was intended to justify the Prophet's desires, why was this limit revealed? Why was Aisha the only young virgin wife? The

Prophet could have married nothing but young, beautiful virgins if he wanted, but instead we see that most of his marriages were for political alliances or for honoring a widow. Remember that he was also the leader of his community. Other tribal chieftains would often have over a dozen wives to seal political alliances, and the Prophet lived in this historical reality. This explains the wisdom behind the allowance to marry more than four wives.

This brings us to the topic of what is revelation and how did the Prophet receive it. Over and over, the Qur'an instructs the Prophet to say to the people, *"I am only human like you."* The only difference between *any* prophet and a regular, noble human being is the revelation the former receives. But what is that revelation? How does it affect a man? We cannot fully answer this because even when the Prophet Muhammad (pbuh) tried to explain what he felt when Gabriel descended upon him, the rich Arabic language was not sufficient to describe the process. Being a prophet does not mean having special powers or sight-beyond-sight; it is a constant struggle to still the inner ego, the inner self, and listen to the promptings of God. Sometimes this is easy, because the issue is important enough for the angel to come down and dictate God's Will to the prophet. However, most times, the angel does not come down, and the very human prophet has to make the best choice they can.

The piece-by-piece revelation of the Qur'an is suited for the kind of interactive dialogue that God intended to happen with his Prophet *and the Prophet's followers.* Often, revelation would come down in response to some problem or issue or question, so the revelations instruct the Muslims who first followed the Prophet and all subsequent generations. This is why sometimes the Qur'an addresses mundane problems like indiscreet children (Surah 24), rude dinner guests (Surah 33), men and women who gossip (Surah 49), and neglectful husbands (Surah 58). Some mundane problems are universal enough and socially disruptive enough to warrant immortalization in scripture. Muslim scholars teach us that this is so all future generations will benefit from these admonitions, regardless of time or cultural background.

Another point is that these constant reprimands to the Prophet highlight the claim that the revelation was not under the control of the Prophet. They could come at any time or not at all. One the one hand, when the Prophet was asked how the Israelites entered Egypt, revelation descended immediately, and the Prophet recited Surah 12 as an answer. On the other hand, the one time that the Prophet implied he would receive revelation when questioned about the Seven Sleepers, revelation did not come for over three weeks. This was an embarrassment for the Prophet, but it showed all those around him that there was no revelation-on-demand. In fact, when the story of the Seven Sleepers was revealed in Surah 18, it included to reprimand the Prophet of his previous statement: **Never say of anything, 'I shall certainly do this tomorrow,' without 'if God wills.' (18:23)**

Finally, Rene, I have attached a free book written by the late Sufi scholar Wahiduddin Khan: *Islam Rediscovered*. Here is a relevant excerpt from this excellent work:

"The Islamic way of life, in a word, is a God-oriented life. The greatest concern of a Muslim is God Almighty. The focus of his whole life is Akhirah, that is, the ideal world of God. He always obeys divine injunctions in every aspect of life. His life becomes a practical expression of the Qur'anic verse: **Take on God's own dye. And who has a better dye than God's? And we are His worshippers. (2:138)**

'Taking on God's dye,' means being of a 'godly character' in all the personal, social and economic affairs of one's life. What kind of character is possessed by this new man is made clear by the following Hadith: **Nine things the Lord has commanded me: Fear of God in private and in public; Justice, whether in anger or in calmness; Moderation in both poverty and affluence; Joining hands with those who break away from me; and giving to those who deprive me; and forgiving those who wrong me; and making of my silence meditation; and my words remembrance of God; and taking a lesson from my observation. *(Razin)"*

May peace be with you,
Ahmed

A New Beginning
Email #12 – From: Rene
Sent: Tuesday, July 25, 2017 7:42 a.m.

Good morning, Mr. Rashed:

Thank you yet again for your responses. I can't express how much I appreciate how much time and effort you have devoted to this. I would like to know how exactly I should go about converting. I have come to this decision after so much reading, learning, researching, thinking, soul-searching, and of course your extensive help and guidance as well. I believe in God and his religion and his prophets wholeheartedly. But I want to go about this the correct way, the way most pleasing to him.

How should I proceed? I have read that one must only recite the Shahada in Arabic in order to become a Muslim; I have read in some places that two male witnesses are required in order for the Shahada to be valid. Is it just as effective for me to say it myself and begin practicing, or is it better to go to a masjid?

I am looking forward to your advice on this matter, and again, I can't thank you enough. May God bless you and your family as well, sir.

Sincerely,
Rene

Email #13 – From: Ahmed Rashed
Sent: Tuesday, July 25, 2017 4:51 p.m.

In the Name of God, the Most Gracious, the Most Merciful

Assalaamu alaikum, Rene.

Welcome to Islam, sister! The Shahada is in the heart and vocalized when the person is ready. The two witnesses is only a formality so new Muslims can get their visa to Saudi Arabia to do their pilgrimage (hajj). However, there are many people who like to make a formal announcement in a mosque as a way to introduce themselves to the community. I suggest you do both…

First of all, if you have no more doubts in your mind or fear in your heart, then go ahead and say the Shahada. God and His angels are your witnesses. Then start practicing; when it comes to practicing Islam, I would recommend two websites (I don't use YouTube too much). This first website is very interactive and easy-to-use, perfect for the new convert:
http://www.newmuslimguide.com/en

For more study and depth, I like this website:
http://www.islamreligion.com/category/55/worship-and-practice/

For step-by-step prayer reference, I recommend the following book by Mustafa Umar:
https://www.amazon.com/dp/B009N4A4MI

Finally, if you have not already done so, try searching for local mosques at this site:
https://www.islamicfinder.org/

When you find one close to you, call them and ask if you can talk to the imam there so you can tell him of your intention to publicly declare your Islam. Usually, he will suggest you come to a Friday prayer to make your declaration with the maximum number of attendees. It is also the fastest way to connect with the active sisters in the congregation. You can also ask about if they have any new Muslim classes or Sisters classes.

I recommend you call several mosques to assess which one has the most convert support (or at least an active women's group). Once you find a mosque that you feel comfortable with, go there and let them know they have a new sister in faith.

As usual, feel free to ask me any questions you have.
May peace be with you,
Ahmed
###

With Dialogue Comes Understanding

A Message From the Author

"You will never understand a man until you walk a mile in his shoes."

I thank you for walking another mile with me on my journey of interfaith conversations. It has always been by belief that understanding comes with dialogue, and I pray this book has added understanding and benefit to you. Since we are at the end of this journey, I would like to share with you some final thoughts. The challenge of modernity and how Islam responds to it is a common line of questions I receive from my students and colleagues. These thoughtful students have read authors like Reza Aslan and Karen Armstrong (among others), and they wonder how Muslims nowadays deal with this approach to Islam from the historical and cultural point of view.

I like to think of myself as moderate and progressive in my thinking while simultaneously religious and devout in my practice. I personally believe in balance between mind, body, and soul. So when I read the cultural and historical writings of these scholars, I feel my faith energized, not threatened. There is always some level of storytelling in religion; yes, even in Islam.

Reza Aslan writes: *Faith is a choice; anyone who says otherwise is trying to convert you. You either choose to believe that there is something beyond the material realm — something real, something knowable — or you don't. If, like me, you do, then you must ask yourself another question: Do you wish to experience this thing? Do you wish to commune with it? To know it? If so, then it may help to have a language with which to express what is fundamentally an inexpressible experience. That is where religion comes in.*

I really appreciate the depths of Aslan's statement here. The stories told about the Qur'an (the Prophet's life, Companions' lives, Hadith, etc.) all revolve around explaining the Qur'an and how it came to prominence in seventh century Arabia. For Muslims like me and Aslan, we accept the divine origin of the Qur'an. This is our touchstone of faith. But when it comes to the hadith and sunnah, there are new ways of viewing them that accepts some findings of modern hadith criticism while maintaining the authority of the Sunnah. The approach I personally use is that put forth by Pakistani scholar Fazlur Rahman. In Daniel Brown's **Rethinking Tradition in Modern Islamic Thought**, he refers the reader to Fazlur Rahman's **Islamic Methodology**: *Rahman opposes any sort of formalistic or literalistic application of hadiths. What is needed instead is "to study hadith in situational context -- to understand their true functional significance to extract the real moral value." The Hadith must be treated as a "gigantic and monumental commentary on the Prophet by the early community." Muslims should study the commentary to in order to apply it directly, but for clues to the spirit behind it.*

So our understanding of hadiths is balanced by considering scientific facts, the historical integrity of contemporary texts, and the culture in which they were written.

As for people like Armstrong, while she sees the impact of the Qur'an, it is not enough for her to personally accept its claims to divine origin. For her, and many other historians, it is just one more example of a human being trying to make sense of the world in their own way. She even says it in one of her books: "Muhammad was creating one of the world's literary masterpieces."

Many people see the beauty and power of the Qur'an but do not see it as something superhuman. This is okay, because from the beginning, that was the defining line between a Muslim and a non-Muslim. This has always been the case. There is always room for doubt. I already accept that, so it does not bother me that there are many secular and historical explanations for religions in general and Islam in particular. The way I see it, since God intended to test people's faith, only those who put their faith in Him via the Unseen will pass this test. So there will never be any irrefutable proof of His existence or of His communication with humanity. While this is a sticking point for my conservative Muslim friends, I believe that eventually this view must prevail in order for Islam to coherently answer the challenge of modernity.

Another line of questions I get often is about the idea that all religions are the result of human evolution. Personally, I believe there is some truth to this, but not in way most people expect. John Bowker writes: *Among the religious world pictures are accounts of what the world or the universe is and of how it began. These are called cosmologies and cosmogonies. Religious cosmologies are not in competition with modern science, though they have often been used or portrayed in that way. If we seek additional information about the universe, we go (if we are wise) to science, not to a religious cosmology. Religious cosmologies serve an entirely different purpose: they show how the universe is as an arena of challenge and opportunity — as much actually for science as for religion. The universe, far from being indifferent to our existence, becomes an invitation to discover its meaning as a demand upon us to act and live in responsible and accountable ways.*

I believe that there IS some reality beyond the material realm. I also believe that this reality has manifested itself to humans since the beginning, but each generation explained and metaphorized that reality in different ways. Those ways are called religions. They differ in how they relate to this Reality, but they relate to the same Reality. Just because I concede that the metaphors and imagery of religions are man-made, that does not mean I think the object of those metaphors are imaginary. The Qur'an says: **It is not for any human that God should speak to him, except by inspiration, or from behind a veil, or by sending a messenger to reveal by His permission whatever He wills. He is All-High, All-Wise. (42:51)**

So even here we see that all inspiration is mediated, not direct. I came to the personal conclusion that at the end we all live and believe according to one dogma or another. Even the secular humanist has a worldview that informs how he or she interprets the world around them, and even nontheists have committed atrocities in the name of their ideology. This line of thinking led me to what I consider the purpose of life's test: Can we use our intellect, reasoning, and free will to *acknowledge* the limitations of our intellect, reasoning, and free will?

One of my favorite authors, Mustafa Akyol, wrote the following: *Religion can work in two fundamentally different ways: It can be a source of self-education, or it can be a source of self-glorification.*

Self-education can make people more moral, while self-glorification can make them considerably less moral.

I have to constantly remind myself and my students that "only God knows best." When a person begins to think or assume that they are free from their ego or self-interest, that is the beginning of their descent into evil. Arrogance and self-righteousness can come from religion, or it can come from hubris. That is why Islam in particular holds me so well. Islam emphasizes "surrender" to God, which often means putting the human being and his intellect and rationalizations and justifications in their place. I find in Islam this constant "chiding" never to assume that your ego will let you go. The great British diplomat, writer, and Sufi Islamic scholar, Gai Eaton, writes about this in his book, *Reflections*. I was really affected strongly by this book. In it, he describes how people have taken the idea of religion and religiosity and "weaponized" it against their fellow man to prop up their own ego and arrogance. This can happen at the individual level, at the communal level, or the political level.

Ironically, the Qur'an actually warns against this in one of the short, early chapters that most Muslims memorize as kids: **So woe to those who pray: those who are heedless of their prayers, who put on appearance, and withhold the assistance. (107:4-7)**

The "assistance" in this verse is commonly understood in the Arabic language as those neighborly acts of kindness and mercy. So we see Muslims who get all caught up in the appearance of piety (prayer, fasting, charity, dress code, etc.) and forget that the Prophet (pbuh) taught that *"Nothing is weightier on the Scale of Deeds than one's good manners."*

Alas, many religious people (Muslims included) are so caught up in their personal and political grief and anger that they do not try to rectify their manners in their personal lives, let alone in their social or political lives. This is the true challenge of modernity: can we as believers combine the ethical goodness that is universally known with the religious goodness that our faith teaches us and call us to implement?

* * * * *

If you enjoyed the book, please spread the word about it to your friends and contacts. If you have the time and inclination, it would be **great** if you would leave a review. Word of mouth is crucial for any author to succeed, so even if it is just a sentence or two, it would make all the difference and would be *very much* appreciated!

You can find more information and updates at our website WhatWouldAMuslimSay.net. Sign up to receive exclusive conversations that didn't make it into the series, free eBooks, my Islam101 slideshows, previews of upcoming books, and other relevant links and resources on Islam.

May peace be with you,
Ahmed Lotfy Rashed

TOUGH QUESTIONS AND HONEST ANSWERS ABOUT THE WORLD'S FASTEST-GROWING AND MOST CONTROVERSIAL FAITH

TOP 15 TOUGH QUESTIONS ON ISLAM

AHMED LOTFY RASHED

Get your FREE copy when you sign up to the author's email list!

**GET IT HERE:
WhatWouldAMuslimSay.net**

MY TEACHER WAS AHMED RASHED. WE SPENT A LOT OF TIME GOING THROUGH THE QUR'AN. AFTER THAT I STARTED TO UNDERSTAND MUSLIMS MUCH BETTER.
—A FORMER ISLAM-101 STUDENT

About the Author

Ahmed Lotfy Rashed was born in Egypt and raised in Maryland. He studied physics at the University of Maryland Baltimore County. While there, he was on the Speakers Bureau for the Muslim Students' Association. He continued his education in Pennsylvania, earning his Masters' degree at Bryn Mawr College.

During his three years of graduate study, he served as Public Relations Officer for the Muslim Students' Association. It was at this time that Ahmed started talking about Islam at various churches, temples, and schools. He became known for his informal and approachable demeanor. His ability to break down complex religious and historical contexts for audiences earned him high reviews. He also taught math and science at the local Islamic School. In addition, he led the Youth Committee of the local mosque in Villanova. Soon after graduating, he married and found employment in Boston as a research engineer.

Since coming to Boston in 2004, he has been an active volunteer at several mosques in the Greater Boston Area. He has been the head instructor for the local Islam101 class since 2006. Also, he has been a volunteer for WhyIslam.org since 2009. He has presented Islam at schools and churches, and he has hosted visits to several major mosques in the area.

Ahmed continues to work and live in the Greater Boston Area with his wife and three children. In his spare time, he likes to read about comparative religions, Islamic law, Islamic history, and military history. He also has a weakness for fantasy and science fiction novels — a problem of which his wife is still trying very hard to cure him.

Appendix A

Preservation of the Prophet's Works & Sayings (Hadith)
AbuIsmaeel Aslam Hussain
www.islamiclessons.com
August 2006

Brief history of Hadith collection, preservation, and classification

Stage One: Time of the Prophet (s)
1. Companions recorded statements and actions of the Prophet (s) — some memorized while others memorized as well as wrote it. An example of such Companions is Abdullah Ibn Amr Ibn Al-Aas.
2. Given the absence of literacy amongst most, they had developed their memory exceptionally well, as that is all they had to rely for most important affairs of their lives as well as for their forms of "entertainment," i.e., poetry. This was further developed due to importance of memorizing the Qur'an and reciting every day in the five time prayers.
3. Practically no Muslim could be a practicing Muslim without memorizing at least some Hadith (statements etc.) of the Prophet — to know what to recite during the compulsory five times prayers, to arbitrate in disputes between themselves at a family level or that of community. So Hadith were indispensable and therefore some memorized by every Muslim.

Stage Two:
Companions (*Sahabah*) of the Prophet Muhammad (s)
1. Efforts of Sahabah in collection for own practice and fatwa for others, e.g., Abu Hurairah (d. 59H), Abdullah Ibn Abbas (d. 68H), Jabir Ibn Abdullah (d. 78H), Aisha bint Abu Bakr (d. 58H), Anas Ibn Malik (10BH-93AH),

Abdullah Ibn Amr Ibn al-Aas (d. 63H), Abdullah Ibn Umar (d. 74H) and Abdullah Ibn Masud (d. 32H).
2. Efforts of Sahabah in ensuring authenticity, e.g., Umar Ibn Khattab and Aisha.
3. They memorized it and some wrote it, e.g., Abdullah Ibn Amr Ibn Aas or their students wrote it from them, e.g., students of Ibn Abbas, Abu Hurairah, etc.

Stage Three:
Tabieen **(Students of the Prophet's Companions)**
   1. **Efforts of Tabieen who devoted their lives at some stage to collection of Hadith**, e.g., Urwah Ibn Zubair (nephew of Aisha), Nafi Mawla of Abdullah Ibn Umar, Thabit Ibn Aslam al-Bunani (spent forty years with Anas Ibn Malik); also Amrah bint Abdurrahman Mawla of Aisha grew up with Aisha learning.
   2. **Written Collection**: Many of Tabieen collected and compiled their Hadith in books that were incorporated in books by the next generation, and most of those that survive today are in that form as part of other larger books.

Stage Four:
Efforts of Next generation after *Tabieen* (*Atbaa Tabieen*)
   1. **Jarh wa Ta'deel**: Assessed soundness of narrators of Tabieen's generation and their own, e.g., Shubah (83H – 160H), Malik Ibn Anas (93H – 179H), Zuhri (d. 124H), Yahya Ibn Saeed al-Qattan (a companion of Imam Malik Ibn Anas).
   2. **Collection of Hadith** from previous generation by travelling extensively to them or spending long time with them, e.g., all of Tabieen mentioned above plus many others such as Ibn Sireen (d. 110H) and Hassan al-Basri (d. 110).
   3. **Compiling and authored books of Hadith** that are still in circulation today, e.g., Malik Ibn Anas, Abdullah Ibn

Mubarak (d. 181 H), Ibn Ishaq (d. 151H). Many others of this and the previous generation (Tabieen) were encouraged (during the first century of Islam) by the Ruler (Caliph) of Muslims then Umar Ibn Abdul-Aziz (d. 101H). Umar Ibn Abdul-Aziz, the Caliph, was himself a leading scholar of Islam.

Stage Five:
Extensive analysis and collections of written works
1. **Extensive travels were undertaken to collect Hadith** and information of *Jarh wa Ta'deel* by personally meeting scholars from previous generation.
2. **These travels were also to meet contemporary narrators** and collect information about them to establish their reliability and trustworthiness. Thereafter, these narrations were analyzed and compared with those of others to determine the extent of accuracy of one's transmission of Hadith.
3. **Scholars who did this included** the likes of Imam Ahmad Ibn Hanbal (d. 241), Sufyan Thawri (97 – 161H), Abdurrahman Ibn Mahdi (d. 198H), Yahya Ibn Maeen (d 233), Ali Ibn Madeeni (d. 234H) and Abu Zur'ah.
4. **These scholars were authorities on classification of authenticity or reliability of a Hadith** — carrying on in footsteps of others from previous generation who were authorities on classifying Hadith in their generation, e.g., Imam Malik, etc.
5. **Some of them compiled books** of Hadith narrations, e.g., Imam Ahmad (Musnad) or books of information about narrators (Ali Ibn Madeeni, Ibn Abi Hatim Al-Razi, and many others) that survive to this day. Other books combined both types or were on one subject but survive today incorporated into other works.

Stage Six:

Further travels and compilation of voluminous books on various topics
1. **Compilation:** Although books were compiled from the first century on a specific topic, now they compiled large voluminous books for a specific purpose but which included numerous chapters.
2. **Examples of these include** Sahih Bukhari and Sahih Muslim by two of the greatest authorities in Hadith. Bukhari (d. 256) and Muslim (d. 261) compiled books on other topics too, e.g., *Tarikh Kabir* by Bukhari with biographies on reliability of narrators (*Jarh wa Ta'deel*). Other authors compiled books for purpose of fiqh (jurisprudence) related Hadith (e.g., Sunan Abu Dawud) or for information about scholars fiqh opinions and its basis, along with authenticity of Hadith (e.g., Sunan Tirmidhi). Many were same Hadith with different chains.

Stage Seven:
Books on various aspects of these Hadith
1. *Fiqh* **(jurisprudence) books:** These used the above Hadith to draw fiqh rulings from them, e.g., al-Umm of Imam Shafiee, some works of Muhammad Ibn Hassan Shaibani, Ibn Mundhir, Muwata of Imam Malik, and many others
2. **Hadith explanation books:** These explained meanings of Hadith from the above books. This continued for many centuries thereafter. Examples include *Sharh Sunnah* of Imam Baghawi, *Sharh Sahih Muslim* by Nawawi, *Fath Bari* of Ibn Hajar, *Sharh al-Muwata* by Zarqani, and many others.
3. **Meaning of wording of Hadith (*Gharib Hadith*):** These were written from the earliest times. Scholars traveled to Arab tribes to establish original authentic meanings of Hadith words. Early works include those of Qasim Ibn Salam. Ibn Athir collected information from these earlier works into a large one work that encompassed books of

the earlier times. This is titled *an-Nihayah fee Ghareebil-Hadith*.
4. ***Jarh wa Ta'deel***: Large books with information from earlier works on biographies of narrators. *Tahdheeb Kamal* by al-Mizzi, *Tahdheeb-u-Tahdheeb* by Ibn Hajar, *Taqreeb-u-Tahdheeb* by Ibn Hajar, are all on narrators of the six books. *Tajeel Manfa'ah* by Ibn Hajar and *Kashif* by Imam Dhahabi are two examples of books of narrators from Hadith present in other collections.
5. ***Takhreej***: These books collected information about various narrators of the same Hadith in order to analyze them and establish their authenticity. Some of these were based on Hadith that are included in works of fiqh, e.g., *Talkhees-ul-Habeer* by Ibn Hajar, *Nasb-ur-Raya* by Zaylaee, etc.
6. **Other books**: **(a)** *Mawdooaat* by Ibn Jawzi (written in 595H) and other such books list fabricated false Hadith (*mawdoo*) for alerting people to them. ***Ahaadith-ul-Ahkaam* (fiqh related Hadith):** Bulugh-ul-Maram by Ibn Hajar.

www.ingramcontent.com/pod-product-compliance
Lightning Source LLC
Chambersburg PA
CBHW070429010526
44118CB00014B/1961